Buckle Up!

*The 5 year journey to the
end of a 100-mile foot race.*

Richard Meston

First paperback edition April 2022

(Amazon) ISBN: 979-8-4237-3534-0

Independently published

For Eva, Sophie, Harry and Oz
for putting up with me banging on about the Arc for 4 years!

Table of Contents

Acknowledgements

There's quite a few people I'd like to thank for the experiences I've written about in this book.

First, there's my family. The poor buggers have had to put up with me for starters, then for the last 4 years have had to endure my obsession with the Arc and me disappearing off each January to have another go. Thanks for sticking around!

Pat Robbins need a mention for putting the whole silly idea in my head to start with and being someone to pester for advice, and Mark Smith for pointing out everything I ever do wrong, which occasionally helps!

Thanks also to Ferg, Jane and Andy at MudCrew for putting on this whole race, a monumental achievement each year and one you should all be very proud of. And of course, a massive thank you to all the Arc Angels who were out on the course for many hours, helping and supporting all the runners along the route.

And a huge thank you to Andy Pridmore for reading through my drafts, spotting errors and suggesting improvements.

arc

/ɑːk/

noun

a part of a curve, especially a part of the circumference of a circle.

of

/ɒv,(ə)v/

preposition

expressing the relationship between a part and a whole.

attrition

/əˈtrɪʃ(ə)n/

noun

the process of reducing something's strength or effectiveness through sustained attack or pressure.

Prologue

I took my first steps from the bright lights of the car park into the darkness with a combination of pride, excitement, apprehension and a heavy mental and physical tiredness.

I'd never been this far in the race before, and the next part was the stuff of legends. What lay before me was continuous hills, mud, rocks, cliffs, wind, rain, incredibly slow progress and the weight of a thousand fears. With more than 65 miles in my legs, and just hitting 24 hours since my alarm woke me the previous morning, I was about to head into the unknown.

To my left was a hill down to the Pendeen Watch lighthouse, and to the right was a pair of boulders clearly marked "Private Property." The route on my watch suggested I add trespass to the list of questionable things you do in the middle of long races, so I headed between the boulders, hoping not to get shot by a grumpy landowner.

As the lights behind faded and the blackness enveloped me, I half expecting to see a sign that read "Here be dragons!"

Let's get this done then…

Introduction

As I sit here, I'm thinking I should probably be doing other things, but instead I'm making a start on my "difficult second book."

This one is about a race - the MudCrew Arc of Attrition. Just a little 100-mile race from Coverack to Porthtowan along the South West Coast Path. A race I've started 3 times before but have yet to finish.

Last time I wrote a book, it ended up being a means of catharsis after an unsuccessful attempt at completing the whole South West Coast Path in 21 days. I'm making a start on this now – a few weeks before the race - as I want it to hold me to account during my fourth attempt at the Arc.

When I'm tired, sore, cold and wet, aching, in pain, limping, hungry, thirsty, dizzy or exhibiting any other symptoms that might be a viable excuse to quit, I'll think about how I'll explain it in the pages of this book. How pathetic it'll sound... unless, of course, I'm crawling up a hill with only one leg still attached, yelling "I WILL NOT GIVE UP!"

So, I've got one rule:

I can stop when
    (a) I get to the end,
    (b) I get timed out, or
    (c) I die.

There are no other reasons. Only being able to see out of one eye, having the use of fewer than two legs, missing an arm… they're all no excuse to stop, and I need to just keep going.

If I don't finish, there won't be a book this year. And I'll have to enter again. And pay for the race and hotel again. And train again. And I'm not sure my family will tolerate *another* year of me banging on about the Arc!

So, I'd better get it done.

See you on the other side!

This book is a bit of a mishmash of things. The first part is me waffling on about my previous running experience, to give some sense of my journey to the Arc of Attrition. Don't be under any illusion that I'm good at this running malarkey, but I have been doing it for a while and it's worth setting the scene.

The second part is the details of my 2022 Arc of Attrition race. But I have a real love for the Cornish coast path, so it's also an opportunity for me to dig into more details of a bunch of interesting sights, buildings, history and geography of the areas that particularly interest me. Hopefully you'll find it interesting too!

And the third part is what happened next, an epilogue effectively. That bit's not too long, but it's nice to close a story down. And I've also put in some lessons, a few thoughts and tips on how you might go about finishing the Arc of Attrition.

This book is again another "therapy session" for me, but I hope you find it interesting, and if you're planning on running the Arc in future (you crazy fool!), then useful too.

CHAPTER 1
The Arc of Attrition

Imagine, if you will, a county with 210 miles of coast, stuck on the bottom left corner of an island, next to 3,000 miles of ocean. Now shake it up and down a bit, so that the coastline is far from flat, add a path round the edge and cover it in mud, rocks and mines (the deep ones, not the ones that blow up when you tread on them - that's a bit extreme even for Cornwall!). Choose a 100-mile stretch of the coast path, but one that doesn't have any river crossings – not an easy task in this particular county. Now, pick a time of year – say… January - where the sun sets at 5pm and doesn't rise again until 8am, and all that lovely weather coming in from the ocean is likely to be at its roughest, coldest and wettest. And finally, convince a bunch of people to run the route.

You've just come up with the *Arc of Attrition*. You should be proud of yourself!

You'll need a few more things though…

First, you'll need someone to organise it, which is far more of a challenge than just running the race. And there's no better bunch of people than Ferg, Jane and Andy of MudCrew. You'll also need an absolute shedload of volunteers, willing to stay up through the night, run miles and miles back and forth at checkpoints, cook food, deal with smelly, grumpy runners and generally be an absolute bunch of legends. You should call them *Arc Angels*.

Add a realistic time limit like 24 hours... actually, maybe that's a bit harsh. Let's say 30 hours... hmmm... OK, 36 hours. That's your lot. Tell you what, give everyone who does it under 24 hours a black buckle, under 30 hours a gold buckle and under 36 hours a silver buckle. Make them big and impressive though, all of them!

That should do for now. Let's see how this goes...

The Arc of Attrition starts in Coverack, about 10 miles east of the Lizard Peninsula on the south coast of Cornwall. The route takes competitors west past Lizard Point and on to the first checkpoint at Porthleven, about 25 miles into the race. Onwards another 15 miles to Penzance – the second checkpoint – and then a further 15 miles through the increasingly tough terrain around Mousehole, Lamorna and Porthcurno, the majority of competitors arrive at checkpoint 3, the Land's End Hotel, in the early hours of Saturday morning. From here, the westward journey finishes and the route turns north through mining country passing Sennen, Cape Cornwall and on to Pendeen. Turning east, the toughest 13 miles of the course take runners to St Ives and checkpoint 4, just before 80 miles into the race. The final 22 miles pass through Hayle, Godrevy and along the North Cliffs through Portreath to finish in the village of Porthtowan.

On the evening of the 6th February 2015, 53 people stood on the start line of the first Arc of Attrition. Cold but otherwise fairly pleasant conditions saw 32 finishers cross the finish line, led over by Steve Wyatt and Duncan Oakes in a tad under 23 hours.

In 2016 the second Arc changed to a midday start and was gate-crashed by a lady called Imogen[1] - much to Ferg's delight, I'm sure - who brought 80mph gusts and generally caused absolute havoc in Cornwall. The field had grown to just over 100 starters, but the tougher course conditions and storms through the race meant only 28 finished. This time, 4 crossed the finish line together: Steve Wyatt, Duncan Oakes, Pat Robbins and Jason Lewis in a new course record of 22 hours 44 minutes, knocking 4 minutes off the previous time.

Now, he won't like this, but I'm going to do a bit of a name drop. I run with Pat Robbins most weeks for a gentle 10 miler on a Monday (well, it's gentle for him, less so for me). He's a thoroughly nice bloke, very humble, and a ridiculously good endurance runner. And I blame him entirely for me spending 4 years trying to complete the Arc... despite the horrible conditions endured that year, he made it sound fun!

---

[1] Storm Imogen hit on 7-8th February 2016, bringing winds of up to 96mph, cutting power to 19,000 people and causing an estimated £80million of damage

14

2017 came along with 109 starters tackling Cornwall's brutal but beautiful coast path. As was becoming a habit, Steve Wyatt crossed the finish line in a new course record of 21 hours 25 minutes, joint first place with Paul Maskell.

Something special happened in 2018. Some bloke called Rich Meston was on the start line for the first time. It was pretty muddy that year as I recall, and from around 150 starters just 52 people finished, the first of which was Mr Steve Wyatt in 23 hours 44 minutes. It must have been tougher conditions that year, with the slowest finishing time so far by almost an hour.

The 100-mile Arc of Attrition race had gained quite a bit of attention by 2019 and a sibling had arrived in the form of the *Arc 50*, covering the 50 miles of the second half of the 100 course and starting on the Saturday morning. On the start line of the 100-mile race was Kim Collison: fell runner, adventure racer and record holder for Hardmoors, Lakeland 100 and Lakes in a Day amongst other high-profile achievements. With a map in hand for the whole 100 miles, Kim took the win, smashing the course record down to 20 hours and 34 minutes. Steve Wyatt took second place in 22 hours 23 minutes, with 67 people finishing. For the second time, I wasn't one of them.

In late 2019, a virus was doing the rounds in China and starting to make headlines around the world. By March of 2020, most of the planet was locked down, but a few weeks before, a little over 220 people stood on the start line of the 100-mile Arc race. Steve Wyatt got his crown back with a fifth 1st place finish in a personal best of 21 hours 24 minutes. There were 111 finishers, and again, I hadn't read the memo properly and forgot to get to the finish line.

There were no Arc of Attrition races in 2021 due to Covid, and I'll leave the race history behind as we head into 2022…

PART 1

History

CHAPTER 2

Banging On About Running

I've been running for a long time on and off, but I don't want you to get the impression that I'm any good. I wanted to take this opportunity to set the scene, and also to self-indulgently waffle on about my background for a bit. Apologies in advance…

How it all started

The year is 1994. I'm at university in Brighton. I've got no lectures today, I'm sitting in my room wondering what to do having exhausted my supply of biscuits, lager and things to do on my rather epic 386 PC. My sister does this funny thing called "running", and I really was *very* bored… I wonder what it's all about.

So, I put on some "fashion trainers" (not running shoes - I don't own any of those), shorts and a t-shirt and head out the door. As an engineering student, I spend most of my spare time sitting in front of a computer or in a pub, so I'm not exactly built for running. I don't go far, and I go far too fast so I'm gasping for air within a few minutes. But I got to the park that's always taken 15 minutes to walk to - only in half the time. I run/walk my way back (well, mostly walk if I'm honest), but in between the aching legs and the straining lungs, the little shard of possibility is glinting in my brain - if I can figure this running nonsense out, I could actually *get* places.

The problem is, I didn't like putting effort into anything physical. I didn't like the discomfort. I didn't like the boredom of doing the same routes again and again. So, I didn't train much, and it didn't get easier.

But I couldn't quite leave it alone.

Progression

After I finished at university, Eva - my girlfriend at the time (and now long-suffering wife) - and I stayed with my sister in Aylesbury. Living in the same house as someone who keeps going out for runs is a good motivator, so we both ended up out and about a few times a week.

Tentatively, we entered our first ever race - a 10K - in 1998 and finished in just over an hour.

I still wasn't convinced about this running malarkey, but it was a good excuse to let me do more of one of my favourite hobbies - eating! When my sister suggested we enter the 1999 London Marathon, which she'd done a few times before, it seemed like a very silly but somehow brilliant idea.

What interested me about running at the time was short, fast stuff - the sort of thing that was over and done with inside half an hour at most. Don't get me wrong, I wasn't in any way fast - I was pleased if I could get a 5K done in half an hour. But I just preferred the feeling of running faster, pushing harder, and getting it done quicker.

With that in mind, it wasn't a surprise that I bloody hated marathon training. Anything over about 3 miles was a long run in my book, and by 10 miles pretty much every time I was throwing my toys out the pram, complaining and generally making it miserable for anyone else around me.

We did a half marathon as a training run in Dorset sometime in early 1999, and the story was the same. I was walking up hills 10 miles in, complaining about how shit running was. We eventually crossed the finish line in about 2 hours 20 minutes.

The London Marathon came around, and there was a level of excitement which I enjoyed in the whole event. It's such a big day out, you can't help but enjoy the razzmatazz. I started at the back of one of the pens - I mean pretty much *right* at the back, next to Chris Chittel who played Eric Pollard in Emmerdale at the time, and somewhere around a bunch of people dressed as trees.

A buzz went through the crowd as the start time passed and due to the mass of people it took a good 10 minutes to get to the start line. Something a little over 2 hours later, having been left behind by a big bunch of running trees miles before, I was crossing the halfway point around Tower Bridge. I was falling apart. Running had become run/walking, and then became almost entirely walking. I walked quickly, covering 13 miles in under 2½ hours, bringing my finishing time to 5 hours 23 minutes. I also decided I was never doing a marathon ever , ever again.

I pretty much stopped running at that point and got on with eating. I got married. We bought our first house. I went abroad a few times on work trips, and while in a Las Vegas hotel in early 2002 I found out my wife was expecting our first child.

Something clicked a bit with running during that year for a couple reasons.

I'd designed and made a little GPS running logger. It was a small box you wore on a belt, and a wire up to a little unit that sat inside a hat, the whole thing logged up to about 4 hours' worth of data as you ran. Once back home, you downloaded the data to a computer and could see speed, elevation, the route on a map etc. Bear in mind this was 2002 - a year before Garmin released their first running watch, and 3 years before Google Maps was a thing… I was quite ahead of the curve with that one! The only way to test it was to go for some runs, so that got me out in a nice, pressure free mood with no real target other than logging data and I found that quite enjoyable.

But the main reason - the one that got me out 3 or 4 times a week, more than I'd ever done before - was that I didn't want to be a "fat dad". Now, we can all pull apart the thinking behind that, but at the time it was an excellent motivator for me.

I used to run the same route pretty much every time. I kept a diary, and over that summer my times dropped along with my weight, and I was getting a real sense of satisfaction in seeing the improvement I was making. This was the first time that I realised there could be some enjoyment in running, albeit a strange, hard-work kind of enjoyment. I think that says a lot about why I ran back then – it seems to have been for the process, the analytics, and the measurable improvements to various physical metrics.

Over the next decade or so, I kept running while I enjoyed it, and stopped when I didn't. I did a few fairly long charity cycle rides - 60 miles and 100 miles - which I enjoyed as a "day out", an adventure in its own right, irrespective of time. And spurred on by my sister, I did another couple of marathons, bringing my time down first to 4:29, then to 4:20 by 2011.

But she went and did something really silly in March 2008. Something called the Jurassic Coast Challenge - 3 marathons in 3 days over the very tough terrain of the South West Coast Path from Charmouth on the Devon/Dorset border to South Haven Point near Poole.

Again, ahead of the times, I'd knocked together a GPS tracker out of some old components I had lying around, and she had it tucked away in her bag. This meant we could figure out where she was and pop up at various points on the route, yell encouragement and hand over sweets and drinks! It was exciting to watch, she battled with the hills and atrocious weather on the second day, and it was amazing to see her finish this quite frankly unfathomable task. Despite this, I had absolutely no interest in doing anything like this. Ever!

Alongside the Jurassic Coast Challenge was another event called The Oner. It took the same route, but all in one go. 82 miles of tough terrain, with a 24-hour time limit. Who in their right mind would even contemplate that? It was absolute insanity!

Ultramarathons

I'd fallen out of love with running again. One February while suffering from a bit of man-flu and lying on the sofa, I started reading the very popular (at the time) book *Born to Run*. For those who haven't read it, it's about ultramarathoning and barefoot running, winding in the story of a South American tribe that took running back to its basics and were incredibly good at it.

The thing that struck me after reading the book wasn't that barefoot running was a great idea (although I did end up getting a pair of Vibram FiveFingers[2] which are still in a cupboard somewhere), or anything really about the biomechanics of running or how our bodies are designed to run. No. The thing that struck me, for some reason, was this: *if you slow down, then in theory you could go on forever.*

---

[2] FiveFingers are ultra-minimal shoes with no cushioning and 5 little pockets for your toes to sit in, much like gloves for your feet. They are intended to mimic running with no shoes on, but giving protection from stones etc on the ground.

Not literally, obviously. But it was a mindset change from me trying to run a faster and faster 5K. How far could you go if speed wasn't even a consideration?

Having done almost no running for the previous few months, once feeling better from my cold (let's call it what it was) I put on my shoes and headed out. The rule was to keep it slow, comfortable and just go until I was bored. I covered 11 miles, which was quite a long run for me back in those days.

The next day I went out again and ran another 11 miles. Now this was pretty much unheard of. My maximum weekly mileage was about 30 miles back then, and those were few and far between. I'd just covered 22 miles in 2 days.

I had a day off, then went out again. Slow and steady. Keep it comfortable. Seventeen miles later I came back through the front door.

OK, so I ended up on the floor in agony with a piriformis issue, not being able to raise myself off the ground for about half an hour! But that was because I'd just gone from zero to 39 miles - my biggest ever week - in 4 days. And suddenly, I *loved* the idea of a long, slow adventure!

An ultramarathon is defined as any running race longer than a marathon, which gives you a wide range of events. Typically, ultras start at 50K (31.1 miles) and go up to 100 miles, 200 miles and more, including timed races like 24 hour and even 6-day events.

So, after reading that book, doing a few long runs and getting inspired to go on a long adventure, I entered the Green Man

Ultra. In March the following year, I'd be heading off on 45 miles of community trail around Bristol on my first ultramarathon, so I'd better get some training in. I gradually increased the distance of my long runs through the year, and in November I'd worked my way up to a continuous (albeit flat) 30 miles from my home to Ringwood and back on a local trailway.

In January - 2 months before my first ultra of 45 miles - I ran from my home to Winchester, a total of 47 miles. It's a bit unusual to run further than the ultra you've entered in training, but it gave some indication of how I was finally starting to enjoy the longer stuff and doing it for the sheer pleasure of it.

I completed that first ultra around Bristol in a pretty slow 11 hours 24 minutes for a total of 48 miles. It was fairly muddy but nothing I haven't seen many times since. But I enjoyed it and felt a real sense of accomplishment having now finished a real, official ultra!

I got a bit carried away over the remainder of 2014. On a whim, I entered the 3rd day of the Jurassic Coast Challenge (that race my sister had done back in 2008 that I thought was ridiculous at the time), covering a hilly 28 miles. I then ran the XNRG Pony Express in May - a 60 mile ultra in the New Forest over 2 days.

My cousin had taken part in Endure 24 the previous year, and so this year I'd entered it as well. It's a 24-hour event where you run round a 5-mile country loop as many times as you can in 24 hours. I thought this would be a good opportunity to get to 100 miles for the first time - 100 miles being a sort of benchmark milestone in longer distance ultrarunning. Although an ultra is technically anything over 26.2 miles, I had come to see 100 miles or more as a "proper" ultra.

As a training exercise I spent 12 hours running around my local country park, racking up just under 56 miles. At the end of June, I went to Reading and set off at Endure 24, with that aim of 100 miles in my head. It all went well for 35 miles (7 laps), then the wheels started falling off. I'd messed up my nutrition, I misjudged the weather and got completely soaked on a lap and all my toys came flying out the pram. I told the race to piss off, got into my tent and went to sleep. An hour later, I woke up again feeling refreshed, at least mentally. The rain had stopped, I grabbed a bite to eat and headed out again, much calmer and just for the fun of the night loops. I had another rest in the morning, but overall managed to get 75 miles in the bag. It wasn't the 100 I'd hoped for, but it was the longest I'd ever run.

In October, I ran the Bournemouth Marathon. Being an "ultrarunner" now, a marathon would be easy. Going in with a confidence I didn't deserve to have, positive mental attitude left the room at about 23 miles, and I ended up turning my watch off in a tantrum and walking a couple of miles. When I crossed the finish line, the time was 4:01:46, and those 106 seconds really pissed me off. I really should be capable of a sub-4 marathon, and I vowed to make a change.

I chatted with some friends who were far better at running than I was to try and figure out how to get better. This was the first point where I actually tried to *understand* running, to try and figure out what was important to get you faster, a bit more than my current training which consisted of planning to "run lots" and actually "not running very much".

I came across *Hadd*[3] training, which, like the *Maffetone*[4] method, involves doing a lot of work at a very low effort level. The idea is that you become much more efficient at using oxygen. Changes occur at a physiological level; you produce more mitochondria and a given pace starts to feel genuinely easier. Well, that sounded brilliant, so I stuck my heart rate monitor on and got to some very slow running.

It was very annoying. Every time I met a hill, I had to walk to stop the heart rate buzzer going off on my watch, and my average pace for runs was about 11-minute miles. But after a few weeks, I noticed that for the first time, I was getting back home after 5 or 6 miles feeling completely fresh, like I hadn't even been for a run.

I stuck at it, and a few months later that 11-minute mile pace had dropped to below 9-minute miles for the same heart rate, and a very similar effort level. And on the rare occasion I stretched my legs on a speed session or a parkrun, it felt genuinely easier to go faster. It really was working!

---

[3] Take a look at hadd.run on the internet for Hadd's "One Approach to Distance Training".

[4] Devised by Dr Phil Maffetone, his method designed to improve aerobic function suggests running at a maximum heart rate of "180 minus your age", so for a 40-year-old, you should run at a maximum of 140bpm.

Going into 2015, I did more of those longer runs. A solo 30 miler in January, a 27 miler in February, and the Green Man Ultra again in March knocking 2½ hours off my previous time, finishing in 8 hours 50 minutes.

A few weeks later I broke 20 minutes at parkrun (5K) for the first time ever.

I ran a solo 40 miler in April, then in May on a solo marathon-length run I smashed my PB by 24 minutes bringing it down to 3 hours 37 minutes. In June, I went back to Endure 24, this time getting that 100-mile distance for the first time taking just over 24 hours (even though it's a 24-hour race, you finish the lap you're doing at 24 hours so your total time can be a little more).

August had me finishing a reasonably hilly 50K in just under 5 hours, and in October I had another bash at the Bournemouth Marathon, getting my (still current) PB of 3 hours 26 minutes.

Things were really exciting for me at this time - my running was improving all the time and I was loving the feeling of getting faster and better!

But my heart wasn't in the road running, I wanted to be doing trail ultras. I wanted adventures!

In 2016, I entered my first 100-mile point-to-point race, the Centurion Thames Path 100, which I completed in around 23 hours 30 minutes, getting the coveted "100 Miles - One Day" buckle and breaking 24 hours for the first time. I did a couple more local marathons or 50Ks, but I was only really interested in the longer stuff now.

Logistically, with a family, it was a bit difficult to disappear off on runs for great chunks of time, so my wife and I came to an agreement that I could do 2 or 3 "big" events in a year. It was a good idea too - I've seen so many people get obsessed with ultra-distance events (like I was beginning to), do too many and a year or two later they're burnt out physically and mentally. I wanted to keep doing this for years, and if it meant just one event a year, then so be it.

In 2017, I ran the Centurion South Downs Way 100. Despite it having 12,000ft of climb, it was very runnable, and I got my 100-mile PB on that course at 22 hours 51 minutes. As had become a habit, I did a parkrun a couple of weeks after the 100 and brought my time there down to 19:02.

Now was time to up the ante. I wanted something tougher. And the one race that had burrowed its way into my consciousness since I'd first seen it 10 years before was The Oner. 82 miles, seriously tough terrain, 24-hour time limit and greater than 50% DNF[5] rate. I paid my money, and I was in.

But it was not to be. We had the opportunity to go to Tenerife over the Easter holiday, a holiday that we as a family would absolutely love. The dates of the school holidays meant there was no way I could do both The Oner and the holiday, and I wasn't going to suggest my family should stay at home just so I could go for a run, so I cancelled my entry and looked for something else.

---

[5] DNF means Did Not Finish. It's commonly used as a verb, i.e. "I DNF'd that race."

A friend of mine called Pat, who I've mentioned before, had done this race called the Arc of Attrition the year before. When I say "done", I mean he was one of 4 people who crossed the finish line in first place in what I think is universally regarded as the toughest year so far. He made it sound fun, and it was at a time of year that wouldn't clash with any holidays. Yeah… what the hell… let's do that one instead…!

2018: Arc of Attrition, Take 1

On the 9th of February 2018, I toed the start line of the Arc of Attrition for the first time. Over the preceding months, I had researched and ended up, in my mind, building this race up to be an absolute behemoth, an impossibility for someone as inexperienced as myself. It was a muddy year. There would be diversions. There were rocks and cliffs. It was a long, long way! By 5 miles in, I'd talked myself into only running as far as Land's End. Sometime after checkpoint 1 at Porthleven, just 25 miles in, my brain gave up. What was I doing? I didn't even like mud! Stupid race. I trudged to Penzance with quads that hated me, made up a whole list of feasible sounding excuses as to why I couldn't go on and waited to be timed out, vowing to pick easier, not muddy races in future.

I think entries opened again about 3 weeks later, and I was probably one of the first in, such is the strange nature of the Arc.

In the spring of 2018, my cousin was walking the whole of the South West Coast Path, aiming to cover the whole 630 miles in about 22 days but spread over a few months. I joined him on a couple of days to cover some of the Arc sections I hadn't seen before. We ran the opposite direction to the race, the first day was 35 miles from Portreath (about 5 miles from the end of the Arc) to Pendeen, and then a further 22 miles on to Lamorna (about 5 miles further on from where I'd ended my race earlier that year) on the second day. It was good to see the course in daylight, and to finally experience the fabled "difficult" bit between St Ives and Pendeen. After this day I described it as "brutally annoying" rather than particularly horrible, but I was on pretty fresh legs, and it was in a relatively dry April... not a very soggy January.

Sometime in the spring, I'd happened across low carbohydrate/high fat eating too. My research into what makes a good ultrarunner found the idea that if you can train yourself to burn fat, you've tapped into a huge energy store. Even skinny people have tens of thousands of calories available in their body... and I wasn't remotely skinny! Off I went into the world of low-carb and keto, much to the annoyance of the rest of my family.

But it definitely helped. For starters, I lost over 10kg without even trying, and that in itself will make you faster at every distance[6]. And I found I could eat a lot less while doing long runs, as long as I kept the pace down.

---

[6] There's a general rule that you will get about 2 seconds faster per mile for every pound of weight you lose, so my 10kg loss should – in theory – make me 44 seconds faster per mile. That's over 2 minutes quicker for a 5K, and almost 20 minutes faster for a marathon!

I did a few more solo marathons, ran the North Dorset Village Marathon in around 3 hours 30 minutes with no specific training, and had the Wendover Woods 50 race on the calendar for November as a training run for the Arc a few months later.

The Centurion Wendover Woods 50 is a looped course consisting of 5 x 10-mile loops. Each loop has about 2,000ft of climb, and some of the hills are tough buggers! It's certainly not an easy 50 miler, and I figured it would be great training for coast path running. But I didn't get to the full 50 miles. When I started pissing blood at 30 miles, I figured it might be a good idea to stop, and the medics on site agreed.

I had some unpleasant investigations after this, and it was diagnosed as "exercised induced haematuria". Basically, some unknown internal bits were rubbing together and bleeding a bit - nothing serious as long as it doesn't keep happening. And I found that if I kept drinking and didn't get too dehydrated while running, it pretty much stays away.

2019: Arc of Attrition, Take 2

On 31st of January 2019, I drove to Cornwall to toe the start line of the Arc of Attrition for the second time. This time, I was ready! I had my targets, deliberately chosen to be a little pessimistic in order to keep me happy and motivated (assuming I was ahead of them of course).

I had been low carb eating for almost a year now and was really reaping the benefits. Long distance running felt easier, and

I could get away with eating far less while doing the longer training runs. My mood was also far more stable day-to-day, generally more positive.

All I had to do was get to the start at Porthtowan. The weather gods tried their best to stop me - and everyone else - by dumping a shit-ton of snow onto the A30. For me, it meant a 2-hour delay to my journey and some cautious driving over the white stuff. For others, it meant an overnight stay on the floor of a local inn, and not getting to their hotel room until 5 or 6am on race day - definitely not an ideal start to a 100-mile race.

With patchy snow on the ground, at 12pm on 1st of February 2019 I headed off on my 2nd attempt at the Arc. It could not have had a more different experience from the previous year. I ought to add the "rose-tinted" warning to this because I'm sure it wasn't all like this, but I remember this being the *best race I've ever had*. Every timing point was being smashed; I was hours ahead of my target time at the first aid station in Porthleven. In the difficult section between Mousehole and Lamorna (around 45 miles in) I was singing out loud, grinning like a lunatic, overtaking everyone I saw and literally bounding and skipping over rocks and boulders. I was having the time of my life!

A niggle in my knee at about 52 miles got me thinking I'd have a word with the physio at Land's End, just a few miles later, and get it sorted. I didn't give it much thought really, until the physio diagnosed it as bursitis and told me there was nothing that he could do, and it would just continue to get worse. Meh, whatever,

I was having fun, it would be fine! A couple of paracetamol downed and I was out the door, albeit with a slightly dodgy gait.

By the time I reached Pendeen, about 10 miles later, I couldn't bend my right leg, my left leg had had enough of being the only thing powering me up hills, and I was about to enter the difficult section - Pendeen to St Ives. I was still happy, I was still enjoying myself, but I didn't want to be a burden calling out a rescue party in the least accessible place on the course if my leg actually packed up completely, so I made the decision to DNF there. I was a sad to not see it through, but it felt like the right thing to do.

Later that year, I had a go at pushing my distance with the 145-mile Kennet and Avon Canal Race. It was as flat as a pancake compared to the Arc - there's more elevation in the first 7 miles of the Arc course than there is in the whole of the Kennet and Avon Canal Race!

A hot July day saw me heading off on the canal race with a 25-minute run/5-minute walk strategy which lasted me over 12 hours. At just about the 70-mile mark, my ilio-tibial band (ITB) decided it didn't want to play anymore. In the space of about 100 metres, I went from being able to run without any issue to my knee being locked up and not being able to run at all (and yes, it was the same knee as before, but a different symptom). After thinking the bottom had fallen out of my race again, I tried some experimentation and found that after a short time I could still walk without any issue. Every time I tried running, the knee locked up again, so I gave up with the idea of running and resigned myself to walking in the last 75 miles, which I did in a pretty decent time. I came into the finish at Paddington in 35 hours 45 minutes, 6th place of the 24 people who finished. There were 42 DNFs, I think mostly down to the heat of the day before. That's by far my best place in a race ever, and I'm proud of that one!

I ended the year with another go at Wendover Woods, this time completing the course in just over 10 hours.

2020: Arc of Attrition, Take 3

On the 31st of January 2020, I toed the start line of the Arc of Attrition for the third time, just before the world started locking down due to Covid-19. This was becoming an expensive habit. Time to sort this blighter out and get on with my life.

Right from the start, it didn't feel as good as the previous year. The enjoyment of 2019 was always going to be a difficult feeling to recreate, and I think that high expectation amplified any discomfort. To top it off, my glasses broke just around 10 miles into the race, so I had to run the rest without any. My sight isn't too bad without my glasses on, but it was more just another annoyance, another thing to dwell on.

On reviewing the numbers, I was actually going a little faster than 2019 for most of the race... until sometime after Penzance when exactly the same thing happened to my knee as the previous year. It was a bit earlier on the course than before, and the fact it happened at all was a real mental blow. I hadn't expected to have the same problem affect me two years in a row, and it seemed to degrade a lot quicker than last time. The few miles from the halfway point to Land's End seemed to take hours, my mood sank and cemented my decision to bow out my 3rd attempt at Land's End after around 57 miles.

I decided after this one that I'd had enough of the disappointment. I was going to finish the Arc one day, but I needed a year off, a mental break, and an opportunity to try and diagnose and sort out my knee issue.

As it happens, the universe agreed.

2021: Cancelled

In 2021, there was no Arc. Some pesky virus had decided to bother the whole world, and the race (which I hadn't actually entered) was cancelled.

I ran round in circles a lot in 2021 and managed to get my 5K time down to an unofficial 18:56 in April, but that was about the only running thing of note.

My motivation for running was fairly low with no events on the horizon for the foreseeable future, but I had come up with a plan to walk the whole of the South West Coast Path in 21 days. The total distance is around 630 miles, and elevation is approximately 120,000ft, so 21 days is a challenge: 30+ mile days with an average of about 6,000ft of climbing. To make it harder, I was going to be self-sufficient, carrying a tent and sleeping gear and finding places on the path to wild-camp as and when I needed. Training involved running a bit and walking a lot with a bloody great pack on my back!

As it happens, that didn't work out quite as well as I'd hoped, but I did enjoy myself. So much so, I wrote a book about it[7]…

I was back from that endeavour by mid-September, and with no focus other than The Oner a good 6 months from then, I ate too much, drank too much and didn't run very much at all.

Until 1st November at 8:50am. I was sat at my desk at work when I got an email:

Hi Rich,

You have been offered a place to The Arc of Attrition. You can accept this offer by visiting: here.

Your offer expires at 04/11/21 08:50:13 (UK Time).

If you have any questions please get in touch.

Thanks

Mudcrew

---

[7] Shameless self-promotional footnote: if you like this book, have a look at *Half the Path* on Amazon next!

I had 3 days to decide whether to enter; it took about 3 seconds. I have no recollection to this day of adding my name to the waiting list, but I must have had one beer too many at some random point over the previous months and signed up anyway. I phoned my wife to ask if she minded if I buggered off in January for 4 days. She wasn't super-enthusiastic, but said she knew how much it meant to me. And suggested I actually finish the bloody thing this time.

Training

An unexpected 12 weeks until the most important race of your life (i.e., the next one) is quite a motivator to stop drinking, stop eating rubbish and get off your arse.

I even did 10 press ups on the office floor after I'd accepted the place and parted with a tear-inducing amount of money on the race entry and 4 days in a hotel.

Instead of doing the work I was supposed to be doing, I dug out the notes I had from my previous 3 times at the Arc, along with all the timing charts, overviews, calculations, Strava links, GPX files and all sorts of other goodies I'd logged away in Google Drive, then set about analysing the living daylights out of everything, like I usually do.

Oddly though, something was different this time. I... well, I *knew* what I was in for. I knew the details, I knew the timings, I knew the course. The bit I normally try to control - the planning and organising - wasn't really there anymore. Which got me thinking in a slightly different way. I came to a conclusion:

There was absolutely nothing stopping me just getting out there and finishing it this time.

Over the next 12 weeks, I targeted a few specific things. When looking at previous training, I noticed that for 2019 (my best year), I'd gained more elevation during the 3 months before the race than any other year, so that was top of my list. I re-joined the local gym and hammered the living daylights out of a treadmill on 15% gradient. Within a few weeks I was covering 4 miles and an equivalent of 3,168ft of climb in under 50 minutes.

I also tried to drop my carbs back down - it worked well in 2019, but I'd fallen off the waggon over the last year or so and it was time to get back on. Right before Christmas… not a great idea, if I'm honest! It didn't work out all that well, but I tried, and hopefully that would slightly reduce my carb requirement during the event.

I watched a lot of videos about the Arc on YouTube. There are far more available now than in previous years as more people are using GoPro's or equivalent to record their endeavours. They are great not only for learning or reminding yourself about the course, but also for building excitement. Whereas in previous years, I had been primarily *nervous*, this year I was mostly *excited*. I couldn't wait!

The documentation on the website had taken a massive step up, thanks I believe to Colin Bathe. As well as the standard information pack, there was a route description guide which detailed everything from sunset/rise times, through all the key points you could make a mistake with really clear maps and explanations. His work on the GPX file for downloading to watches was excellent, a few minor revisions over the month preceding the race and the end-result was a pretty much spot on track with enough detail to keep you from almost all the sticky situations you could find yourself in.

In those 12 weeks I covered about 700 miles, with 90,000ft of climbing, and about 100-150 miles of fast walking. I'd also convinced myself, mentally, that I could do this. It wasn't necessarily going to be pretty, but there was absolutely no reason I couldn't get this done.

Timing Planning

When faced with a big challenge, I like to try and control everything I can. Whilst things like the weather and condition of the path was totally out of my hands, nutrition and timing was something I could obsess over.

The first time I started the Arc, I just ran. It didn't go all that well, but it laid down a set of splits and overall times to aim to improve upon. By the fourth time, I had things finely tuned… or rather finely tuneable. I had spreadsheets and analysis programs all over the place, I'd downloaded the timings for everyone on the Arc for a number of the previous years, I had elevation plots, split times pretty much to the mile and statistical analysis results for each section.

I'd also written a Data Field for my Garmin watch. Called *UltraTimes*, it added a screen on the watch which showed the timings at set points along the way. Before the race, using my phone, I could program the points and the times I expected to be there.

For the 2019 attempt, I picked a rough set of times that were based on a finish within the 36 hours (taking into account the St Ives cutoff being tight, so having to go at about 34-hour pace for the first 80 miles or so in order to not get timed out). The positivity created during the race by me going faster and being first minutes, then hours ahead of the planned times was amazing!

In 2020, I optimistically pushed things harder, with the 30-hour gold buckle timings in mind, and it didn't go as well.

So, for 2022, my timings were back to a slightly refined version of "getting round", with a target finish time of just after 10:30pm. This would be slow enough that I should always be ahead of the times, thus giving me a positive feeling through the event, but fast enough that I had about a 90-minute buffer if things went very wrong towards the end.

Training done. Timings sorted. Three practice runs at completing the Arc of Attrition… I think it's about time to get on and finish it now!

PART 2

The Arc of Attrition 2022

CHAPTER 3
To Kernow

It was almost time to leave. Everything was packed - and I mean _everything_. I had bags and boxes, my race pack, several rucksacks and sports bags full of everything I might conceivably need to run the race.

Just before heading off, I stuck an obligatory post on Facebook with a tracking link and a bit of my story:

Back in February 2018, I started a race that turned out to be my first ultra DNF.

The race was the Arc of Attrition: 100 miles of muddy, hilly Cornish coast path from Coverack, past the Lizard, Penzance, Land's End, St Ives and on to Porthtowan.

I wasn't ready mentally or physically, and the amount of mud that year just ruined me so I stopped at Penzance, 40 miles in.

I returned in 2019 and had what I still consider to be my best race ever - I remember singing and skipping over boulders while grinning from ear to ear after 45 miles… until a knee injury stopped me at around 70 miles. I was gutted to have to stop, but at the time thought it was the right thing to do.

2020… and my third go at this silly but fantastic adventure. The knee problem came back, only 10 miles earlier this time, and I had to bow out at Land's End after around 55 miles

I didn't bother entering for 2021, I needed a break, and it turns out the world agreed and cancelled the event anyway for some reason I can't quite recall.

1st November 2021, I get an email in my inbox saying a wait list place has become available for the 2022 Arc. I had no recollection of ever putting my name on the waitlist, but maybe one evening after one too many beers I thought it was a good idea?

So I entered. 12 weeks notice. A nice length of time to get training.

And here we are - one day before Kick Off.

Tomorrow at midday, I start my FOURTH attempt at the Arc of Attrition. And this time, I've got this. I have one rule - I can stop for 3 reasons: (a) I finish, (b) I get timed out, (c) I die.

And this time, I'm fully expecting my knee problem to come back - it only shows itself after 50 odd miles, so it's difficult to diagnose! But I'm ready for it this time. I have poles, and expectation of its return, and a mindset to just slowly trudge the second half hopefully within cutoffs.

Let's see if all those good intentions go to shit at 5am on Saturday morning...

At 10:15am on this rather dull Thursday morning, I got into the car and started the drive to Cornwall.

The drive was fairly uneventful. Coming from home near Poole in Dorset, I stopped at Dart's Farm just outside Exeter for a steak pasty and decaffeinated coffee (don't judge me yet, I'll explain the decaf bit later!) and to top up the charge in the car. Then I headed to Lifton on the Devon/Cornwall border for another charge to make sure I had enough to get to the hotel, do the necessary trips back and forth to the race HQ and then get back to a charger. I took the opportunity to go for a wander around Lifton which isn't the most exciting place in the world, and also stopped in the small convenience store to grab a roll of aluminium foil, something I'd forgotten to bring and would need tomorrow.

The weather was grey and cloudy, the roads wet, and a steadily increasing drizzle soaked the windscreen as I drove through Cornwall. All over December, there had been a fair amount of rain and I think the Arc route had got pretty muddy, just how Ferg likes it - after all, why else would you set the race in winter! But the last few weeks had been mostly dry, and in Cornwall at least, quite warm for the time of year. From all accounts on Facebook, the path was in great shape, but if there was a bucket load of rain today, that could change.

I arrived at the Premier Inn in Camborne at just around 3pm, checked into the room and wasted some time until registration opened at 5pm. I lay on the bed finishing the book *Becoming Brutal* by Claire Smith, the owner of Brutal Events and finisher of a double-deca iron-distance triathlon (that's a 48-mile swim, 2240-mile bike ride and 520-mile run... a pretty much unimaginable set of distances!). Whatever I would be going through tomorrow and the day after would be nothing compared to the 28 days of absolute misery Claire suffered during that event. I didn't realise at this point, but she had entered the 2021 Arc event which was postponed, so she would actually be on the start line tomorrow.

I was fidgety, wanting to get on with things and at about 4:30pm, I gave up waiting, headed out to the car and decided I would just sit in the car park until 5pm for registration. The drive took about 10 minutes, and it's one I've done a lot before so I knew the route. When I arrived, the place was already busy with cars, so once parked I got my kit out the boot, headed straight over to the main building and went inside.

Kit check is always a bit of a faff. I knew what was coming, and I really should have had everything easily accessible, but instead I had to dismantle my carefully packed bag to dig out my mobile phone waterproof case, two head torches and spare batteries, survival bag and a few other things. Kit check passed and I got my token, which resembled a casino chip, then quickly stuffed all my kit back in the big carrier bag I was holding and headed over to the numbers table where my race number - 206 - was handed over in exchange for my kit check token.

All done. I milled around a little but didn't recognise anyone to have a chat with, so headed out to the car and drove back to the hotel.

Dinner was booked in the pub next to the hotel for 7pm, so I had a little under 2 hours to kill.

I laid all the kit I was wearing tomorrow out on the floor of the hotel room. From the left were my Saucony Peregrine ST shoes, then a pair of Drymax socks, a pair of Injinji toe socks, my Montane gaiters, a pot of 2Toms Blistershield powder and a stick of Trench foot cream. That's the feet done.

Next was a fetching pair of Decathlon seamless anti-chafe undercrackers, compression shorts, long running tights (which were mandatory kit so if I didn't wear them, I'd have to carry them) and some very light shorts as a top layer. This was where I would have pinned my number had I remembered to pick up some pins from registration! There was also a pot of Squirrels Nut Butter, which stops chafing and goes... well, use your imagination!

For the top half, there was my long-sleeved merino wool base layer (another piece of mandatory kit), a light t-shirt and finally my buff.

I re-packed my race vest – a Salomon Advanced Skin 12 Set - with all the bits and pieces I'd removed for kit-check. In the area against my back meant for an optional water-bladder I had a dry-bag with my second mandatory long sleeved base layer (this one considerably warmer than the other as it would be needed in an emergency), my survival bag, waterproof trousers and a somewhat surprisingly non-mandatory first-aid kit. This was a little bigger than the usual typical runner's first-aid kit of 3 plasters in a plastic bag. Having fallen over a few times over the years, I now carried a useful kit with some dressings, bandages, tape and various other things - the bulk was unnoticeable when in the pack, but I had enough stuff to actually do some decent patching up if necessary.

In the large, main compartment on the back of the race vest I had my main head torch in a plastic bag, and another bag with packs of food to swap to the front at the Porthleven and Penzance aid stations. At the bottom was a drybag with my spare head torch, spare batteries, MP3 player and headphones (plus backup MP3 player and headphones - some things are too important to risk!), a small USB power bank, and charging cables for my watch, MP3 players and phone.

The stuff-pocket at the bottom back of the vest had a big plastic bag containing my waterproof jacket and waterproof shorts (yep, you can get them and they're very useful if it really rains!). The weather looked like I wasn't going to need them, so I wrapped them in the plastic bag so as not to get them soaked in potentially 36 hours of sweating, which probably wouldn't do the waterproof coating much good. The big stuff-pocket also had another drybag with my mandatory waterproof over-gloves, a balaclava (it was light, and useful one year when it was really cold), a spare buff and my pop-up plastic cup.

Finally round to the front of the vest. On the left side stuff-pocket I had my Rab gloves and GPS. On the right, I had a small bag of salt-tablets, and a bigger bag with all the food I should be eating until Porthleven, 25 miles and likely the best part of 6 hours into the race. The only thing missing from the vest was my two soft-flasks, and a third soft-flask that I would stick into the back stuff-pocket to make up the required 1.5 litres of water carrying capacity.

The very last thing was my poles - Leki carbon Micro Trail Pro. These are great poles, but they're slightly different to your standard ones with a wrist loop. They have a special "Shark Glove" which you wear, a kind-of velcro'd on hand-harness rather than a full glove. The poles clip into a tiny but strong loop on the glove between the thumb and index finger. This means you can use your hands easily with the poles hanging, no chance of dropping them when they're clipped on. But a quick-release button on top lets you unhook the poles easily if you need to detach them.

The Salomon vest I have has a special attachment on the shoulders on which you can attach a "quiver" and have access to the poles while you run. I've used it successfully when the bag isn't very full and it's great - you can get the poles out and put them back without stopping running. But load the bag up with as much stuff as I had, and every time I tried the quiver, the shoulder strap would twist, digging into my shoulder to a point where I knew after 10 or 20 miles it would be a big problem, let alone 100 miles. So, my alternative was to leave the poles in the quiver as it's a nice holder for them, but instead of the shoulder attachment I'd use the compression-straps on the back of the vest to hold the quiver flat against the bag. It means there's no way of getting the poles out or putting them back without stopping and taking the pack off, but I intended to carry them to Porthleven (25 miles) and then use them mostly continuously from there.

Phew! Written like that, it sounds like I was carrying an awful lot!

I still had a while until dinner, so I plugged a few gadgets in for a top-up charge, filled up my soft-flasks and left them on the side in the bathroom to make sure there were no leaks. I had spares in the car and I'd rather find a small leak overnight than during the race.

I read a bit more book, then headed down to dinner 15 minutes early to see if the table was free. I was in luck, and within about 30 minutes I'd eaten a steak pie with mashed potatoes, a side of cheesy garlic bread and had my obligatory pre-race pint of Guinness.

Back up in the room, I really had nothing to do other than panic, so despite it being early I had a quick shower and then headed to bed around 8pm. I hadn't been having enough sleep over the previous few nights, so I figured that longer in bed tonight would probably help - if not asleep, then at least I was physically resting. And besides, I wasn't really expecting it to be a great sleep as I was both ridiculously nervous and hugely looking forward to getting on with the race.

Breakfast was booked for 6:45am and I had time to prepare afterwards, so I set my alarm for a rather civilised 6:15am (civilised for race day anyway) and drifted off into a restless and not particularly revitalising sleep.

CHAPTER 4
Race Day

Friday 28th January

My watch and phone alarms went off simultaneously, rousing me from a light sleep. Shit! This was it. Arc Day. The excitement I'd felt up to now was mostly gone, replaced by an overwhelming nervousness.

I got straight out of bed, had a wash and made a cup of the weakest tea ever to try and keep the amount of caffeine down.

It's probably time to explain the slightly odd caffeine situation now: I usually have plenty of coffee and tea, but one habit I've got into before ultras - long ones anyway - is to cut out all caffeine for 2 or 3 weeks beforehand. It's reasonably easy after the first few days, and the boost you get from the cups of coffee or some coke in the race is immense after you've had the break from it.

Tea drunk, clothes on, I headed down to breakfast. Entering the pub where breakfast was served, I waited by the reception desk for someone to show me to a seat. After a few minutes of no-one coming, I wandered into the main area to try and find someone. One lady already seated told me that they were running late and just to take a seat and the guy running the show would come and find me to take the room number.

Despite being open for over 20 minutes now, there was no hot food yet. I'd been sticking to low-carb eating for most of January, and it was a particular part of my routine that on race day I didn't have any carbs until an hour or so into the race to make sure my body was making the most of fat as a fuel. This meant I couldn't go and grab any of the food already on offer – the carb-rich options of yoghurts, fruit, cereal, crumpets, croissants, pastries etc.

About 7am, with me on my second cup of instant decaf coffee (just as delicious as you'd expect), the hot food started arriving. Sausages, bacon, eggs, mushrooms, tomatoes and black pudding should see me right!

Once that lot was eaten, I went back up to the hot plate and got another 2 bits of bacon and 2 more sausages. Back at my table, I liberated from my pocket a plastic freezer bag containing a couple of bits of aluminium foil from the pack I'd bought yesterday in Lifton, wrapped up the bacon and sausages and popped them back in my trouser pocket.

I made a bit of a mistake back in 2018, the first time I'd tried the Arc. I had breakfast before 7am and had completely forgotten that the race wouldn't be starting until 12pm. By the time I started, I hadn't eaten or drunk a thing for 5 hours, and it certainly added to the reasons why that year didn't work out well. Since then, I'd made sure I had something to eat on the coach on the way to Coverack, and also made sure I carried a 2-litre bottle of water around all morning, sipping regularly to keep fluid levels up.

Back in the room for the last time before kick-off, I started the whole rigmarole of getting ready. Pants, compression shorts, leggings, outer shorts, gaiters (remembering, this time, that they have to go on before shoes!), blister powder in socks, Trench cream on feet, Injinji socks on, Drymax socks on top, shoes on, gaiters clipped and velcro'd on. Long sleeved base layer, t-shirt and buff on my wrist. Confirmed non-leaking soft flasks refilled, half a pack of Tailwind (an all-in-one nutrition powder for running) in one of them, two flasks went into the front pockets of the bag and one spare into the stuff pocket at the back with my coat, so I had 1.5 litres of water ready to go.

My plan had been to leave about 8:30am so I wasn't hanging around too long at race HQ getting unnecessarily nervous, but I decided with 250-odd people starting that it was going to be very busy and earlier might in fact be better. I checked the registration time and found it opened at 7am.

A bit before 8am, with my race vest on my back and a carrier bag with 2 litres of water, 2 sausages and 2 bits of bacon inside, I closed the door on my hotel room and headed to Porthtowan.

CHAPTER 5
Race HQ

Mount Pleasant Ecological Park, Porthtowan

Fifteen minutes later, I was entering the Eco Park. I drove through the smaller car park into the main field which was being used as the main car park for the event. I stuck myself in a spot as the first car after a long line of vans.

I have this irrational worry about "the parking". It's a bit of a catch-all for everything that can go wrong on the way to something important - a race, a meeting, a concert etc. Once the car is parked, that bit is sorted and out the way and I can relax. And here I was, parked in a field. Everything that could go wrong before the race had happened. Well... nearly everything.

The boot of the car was filled with all the running related paraphernalia I owned, but right now all I needed was my race vest and my carrier bag containing water and munchable pork products. I wandered up the path, round the corner and into the HQ which was bustling with people. An oil drum with burning wood stood in the middle of the enclosed area, creating warmth and that bonfire smell and giving the whole place a lovely atmosphere.

With my number already in hand I didn't have to do the kit check so headed straight to the back room where the tracker magic happened. For this race, you have a shoulder-mounted tracker fitted which broadcasts your location every minute or so. Not only can the Arc Race HQ keep an eye on you and check you're not trying to take a short cut by falling off a cliff and drifting round in the sea, but family and friends can "dot watch" your live progress via the website at OpenTracking. There's also an SOS button, which you can press if the shit has really hit the fan, like you can't find somewhere that makes a decent espresso on the route. The fitting process is well-honed - a zap of the barcode on your number, and you're linked to a tracker unit which you take through to the next room, and someone tapes it to your vest. 30 seconds is all it takes, and now there's no hiding!

The last job to do – attaching my number. I grabbed some safety pins and tried to stick it to my shorts without stabbing myself. After too many minutes of trying and quite a bit of swearing I gave up, took off the shorts and pinned the number with minimal hassle, then put them back on. That was mostly the point of the shorts after all - it meant I could easily change any other clothes, and just stick these super-lightweight shorts on top and have my number on show, without ever having to fiddle with pins enroute which would almost certainly not have ended well.

Next up, my drop-bag. Unsupported Arc runners - those without a crew on the route to help them - of which I was one, get a bag transported to Land's End. You can put what you like in it as long as it's within the size limit. In a Skechers drawstring bag I had a full change of clothes including a spare pair of shoes, another set of walking poles in case my others were damaged or lost, another USB charger and watch charge cable, more spare batteries, some Squirrels Nut Butter, and all the nutrition I'd need for the section from Land's End to the end of the race.

The official drop bags are nice silver draw-string plastic bags, so I took one, along with a tag to write my name and number on, and set about squeezing my Skechers bag in. It was about 5% too big and after much squeezing I managed to split the silver bag down the side. Like a naughty schoolchild who'd just broken something, I ignored it and worked around the problem. I half emptied my bag into the silver bag, then shoved my now smaller black bag in the top, just as the lady by the desk said it would be fine to just put the tag on my own bag. Bugger! Well, it was done now, so I tied the string in a big knot to stop things falling out, hoping it would be easy to undo at Land's End when I next saw the bag, and handed it over.

While mucking about with the bag I'd noticed Stephen Cousins with a camera. As well as being the guitarist and vocalist in A Tribe of Toffs who had a 1988 hit with *John Kettley is a Weatherman*, Stephen also runs. And his company, *Film My Run*, also sees him... er... filming runs. He's completed the Arc 3 times in decent and progressive gold-buckle times of 29:50 in

2017, 29:15 in 2018 and 28:31 in 2019, and now isn't allowed to run it any more as he's the Director of Streaming Stuff for the Arc of Attrition (don't quote me on that being his official title). And honestly, he does a bloody good job of it.

Having run with Stephen for a bit in the 2019 race, I said a quick hello to him, and in chatting I mentioned it was my 4th start today and hopefully my first finish. "Over here," he said, and pointed to the space in front of the camera. And there it was, my first live interview on TV (well, YouTube, but same sort of thing, right?). We chatted for a couple of minutes about my previous attempts, and how my knee was the cause of 2 DNFs. Stephen suggested that as my knee issue happened shortly after the 7-mile road section in Penzance both times, to take that bit very slowly and be careful as there was a chance it could be a trigger for the issue. A great point, and anything was worth a try, so I logged his advice away for about 12 hours later.

There was still a good 90 minutes or so before the coaches left, and unlike previous years there was no-one I knew here today, so I headed back to the car to have some quiet chill-out time. The stereo in my car isn't bad, so I stuck on some music and tried to relax. I've got a pretty eclectic music taste - everything from metal to classical, hip-hop to jazz - and today I started with something fairly mellow: *One Day Like This* by Elbow. As I got more into it, I turned the volume up. Then it was onto a few things a bit louder, each time I was turning the volume up a bit, and by the time I hit *Solidarity* by Enter Shikari people were looking at the car as they walked by. But what the hell, it worked for me: I was getting lost in the music, and surely just before you run what is one of the toughest 100-mile races in the country you're allowed to do odd things?!

Time went on and I felt slightly nervous of missing something (like the buses randomly leaving an hour early – I'm a worrier!). Unlike in previous years, there was no pre-race briefing so as to avoid an unnecessary mass gathering given the risks still associated with Covid-19. Jane and Ferg had produced a 40-minute video containing all the information needed about the race which has been emailed out to competitors a week or so earlier, and this was playing on a loop in the registration area.

I went back to the HQ area and it was definitely busier now with a lot more people chatting in groups both inside and outside the building. As I walked through the people, I noticed a few with Salomon quivers on their packs, nicely hanging down the side of the pack and not twisting the shoulder like mine had always done. I'm normally a bit socially awkward, but the group-panic of the hour or two before something like this makes everyone friends and I randomly approached a few people asking to look at how they attached their poles to the pack. I got chatting to two guys, one had the poles nicely sat on the back of his pack. I had a look, and wasn't convinced it would work for me, but the other guy mentioned that he was using a Salomon Pulse belt to hold his poles around the back of his waist. I had one of those belts in the back of the car - the advantage of having brought pretty much everything I own that's running related. What harm could it do to go back to the car and get the very lightweight belt to put in my bag, just in case? Well, more than you might expect!

Back at the car, I popped the boot. I dug around in my massive box of running stuff and located the belt. It was one of two I owned, this one being the smaller size. Salomon make this belt in 5 sizes - XS, S, M, L and XL. I bought the S initially (the one I had in the car), and it was a bit tight, so I then bought the M size but that one I'd left at home. It turns out any normal human being probably needs the XL - Salomon do err on the small side. But nevertheless, I got the belt out and stuck it in the zipped part of my bag for use later on. If it worked, great. If not, no big loss, it probably only weighed about 20g.

All done, pack back on my back, I pushed the boot of the car shut. It bounced. I pushed again. It bounced. I repeated this about 5 times. The latch wasn't clicking. This had happened once before in a car park in Salisbury, but I don't remember how I fixed it. I slammed again, and again, and again. An Einstein quote came into my head: "*Insanity is doing the same thing over and over and expecting different results.*" I told my brain to fuck off and slammed a few more times.

The coaches were going in 30 minutes. With the boot not latching, I couldn't lock the car. Also, my car runs on batteries. Leaving the boot open would probably keep the car "on" and I'm not sure it wouldn't be flat 36 hours later. Also, I had laptop, iPad, camera etc in a bag in the boot. Could I leave it unlocked? Well, I wasn't going to miss the bloody race for anything, so yeah,

I could leave it unlocked and deal with it later. But I had a few more minutes at least.

I slammed it a few more times with no success, then dug around in my running box for some tool to poke into the lock. I found my "footcare kit" and started poking the latch mechanism with tweezers, a nail file and a pair of scissors. Maybe a pedicure would convince it to behave. Nope. I slammed it again. Fuck!

Right. Sod it. Leave it unlocked. It's not like anyone would notice, probably. The car did have a "frunk", which is a storage space under the bonnet (it's American, so what we call the "boot" is the "trunk", so the "frunk" is the "front trunk". I suppose the UK equivalent should be a "froot"). At least I knew I could lock that, so I transferred my bag with the laptop/iPad/camera into the frunk and tried clicking the key a few more times. I heard the familiar sound of the latch working, crossed my fingers, grabbed my water & pork-filled carrier bag (if this worked, I wasn't opening it again!), and slammed. YES, it locked!

Well, that had taken my mind off the race for a few minutes! I was relieved, but I wasn't going to touch the car again until after the race.

Back outside the HQ building, a convoy of coaches had arrived, and I milled around aimlessly for a few minutes then wandered down to the front coach and got on. I was early enough to have a choice of almost any seat, and picked one half way down by the window, carefully putting my race vest onto the floor between my legs and sticking my big water bottle in the bungee area behind the seat in front. I took the opportunity to

61

munch a bit of bacon and a sausage, knowing they'd probably smell quite a bit and not wanting to offend anyone who wasn't a fan of meat nearby.

The coach filled up and a guy sat next to me, his wife waving goodbye to him from outside the coach window for a surprisingly long time. I heard a voice I recognised on the opposite side of the coach and a few rows back, but it took a second to place it. I suffer from mild prosopagnosia - "face blindness", or the inability to recognise people when you see them - but I'm pretty good with voices. Then it twigged - it was Tristan Stephenson, from the *Trail & Error* Podcast[8], a firm favourite of mine and regular companion to runs over the last few months since I'd found out about it. Tristan had placed 2nd in the Arc of Attrition in the past, and was likely to do very well today. I'd also had a chat with him on Facebook and he was using my Garmin UltraTimes data field for the race to show checkpoint times, so I hoped it worked OK! He was having a bit of a hard time - it turns out the crew he had sorted for the night time had just fallen through due to Covid, and he was desperately trying to figure out alternative arrangements so was on the phone quite a bit on the coach.

---

[8] OK, promo bit here: I have no affiliation with the T&E podcast, but it's brilliant! The two hosts are Tristan who's a proper speedy ultrarunner with a great analytical mind – and Jay, who I have had the pleasure of an hour or so video call with to try and diagnose my knee problem and is an absolute genius in his field of running operation, maintenance and repair. Highly recommended.

On the route from Porthtowan to Coverack, we passed RNAS Culdrose - Europe's largest helicopter base, and currently hosting the Training and Operation Conversion Unit operating the EH101 *Merlin* helicopter. It's also the base for various Royal Navy Merlin Squadrons, Early Warning and Search & Rescue Sea King helicopters and some Hawk T1 trainer jets, so a pretty important place.

This was a place that held some personal significance for me too. Bear with me as I head off on a bit of a tangent... about 25 years ago, my dad built a plane. Yes, one of the flying ones. He bought a kit for an Avid Flyer, but part way through the build decided the 2-stroke engine used was a bit poxy (and suffered from icing of the intakes which made it likely to stall at under 10,000ft), so swapped it for a much better 4-stroke Rotax engine. This required strengthening of the fuselage and recertification of the whole aircraft, and made it a unique plane, one which garnered quite a bit of interest. He flew for many years in this little thing, and I had the opportunity to go for a few flights, but the time had come over the last year or so to part with his beloved aircraft. Mainly due to Covid, the sale was a pretty long and arduous process, but eventually it went to a bunch of enthusiastic young pilots... based at RNAS Culdrose. I kept an eye out as we went past the incredibly long fence of the air base, but didn't catch any glimpse of Pill[9]. It wasn't the sort of day for flying a light aircraft with all the fog, so I expect it was tucked away nicely in a hanger somewhere.

A little later, I spotted the 1½ miles to Coverack sign and the butterflies fluttered in my stomach. I finished the remaining food I had with me and watched out the window as we descended down into the village.

Coverack (from the Cornish *Porthkovrek*, meaning *cove of the stream*) is a classic little fishing village, a crescent-shaped beach in a beautiful cove. It's got a wonderful feel, with many white cottages with thatched roofs. When the Arc of Attrition isn't starting there, the place is quiet and peaceful, with the sea lapping on the shingle beach. The sheltered bay is a popular place for snorkelling, scuba diving and windsurfing, giving rise to the windsurfing and kayaking centre in the village.

As is common for the villages on the coast in this area of Cornwall, the 300-year-old harbour was constructed for the growing fleet of boats fishing for pilchards. A little north of Coverack are the Manacles, a set of treacherous rocks that have been the cause of over 150 shipwrecks and following the particularly tragic wreck of the *SS Mohegan* in 1898 with the loss of more than 100 lives, an RNLI lifeboat station was opened in Coverack in 1901. It seems that ships got somewhat better at

---

[9] The plane was known as Pill, and I'd heard a couple of stories about why from Dad. First was that "the pill's paid for it" (he was a pharmacist), and second was because he was involved in the development of Sildenafil - aka Viagra - which was nicknamed the "g-pill" in the lab. The plane registration is G-PILL

avoiding hitting the rocks and lifeboats got faster, as in 1972 the one remaining all-weather lifeboat was replaced with an inshore inflatable, and in 1978 it was withdrawn completely, the area now being serviced from Lizard and Falmouth. The old lifeboat house, with its curved metallic roof, is now a fish and chip restaurant.

The summer is busy in Coverack, with the carnival taking place in July, and in August the RNLI Lifeboat Day, Pirate and Mermaid Week and Coverack Regatta. There's also a Christmas Day tradition in Coverack - a bunch of hardy lunatics jump in the water and swim in the harbour in aid of charity, much to the consternation of the villagers and any passing tourists (actually, it seems they all tend to join in!). The tradition has, apparently, gone on for more than 50 years and raised a lot of money for Cancer Research.

We passed the car park where everyone gathers for the start, and I was surprised at just how many people there were. I'm sure in previous years the entry count was more like 150-200 people, but this year the Arc is a qualifier for Western States[10] which imposes a requirement for a minimum number of starters and the whole place was chock-a-block.

I left the coach and walked back up to the car park. Across the entrance was a huge inflatable Raidlight branded start gantry,

---

[10] The *Western States Endurance Run* or *Western States 100* is widely considered the first ever 100-mile ultramarathon. Taking place in the Sierra-Nevada mountains, it's a bucket-list race for a lot of runners. Entry is via a ballot and to get a ticket to the ballot you need to have completed a qualifying race.

and just behind this a van with a large set of speakers blasting out music and Stephen Cousin's commentary about competitors and the race in general. It's a great atmosphere at the start, there's no doubt something big is about to happen!

Having been here a few times before, I had a routine. Fifteen minutes or so until the start, I headed up to the back of the car park to use the toilets for the last time. I finished my water bottle and put the rubbish I had in the now overflowing bin and headed back down to nervously soak up the atmosphere until we headed off.

Stephen was interviewing runners who were expected to do well. All the interviewees were being very humble and cagey about their targets, most saying that they "just wanted to finish".

With a few minutes to go, I headed a little nearer the start. Now, for a very-much mid-pack runner, it's usually not a good idea to get carried away with the pace nearer the front of a race. But I knew a few things about this one that made me think it would be a good strategy. The first few miles were mostly narrow single-track trail and there's not a lot of overtaking opportunities, so it's better to be somewhere nearer the front rather than in a big queue at the back. There's also the state of the ground - if only 50 or 60 pairs of feet have gone over the muddy trail, it'll be easier going than if 300 pairs of feet have done the same.

Time ticked by, and the commentary stopped and was replaced by Keith Hill beating a huge drum to music, a cover of Led Zeppelin's *Kashmir*. Keith recalls a story about the music:

A small bit of unknown history to using this track. It's a great track! When Ferg and I were discussing start sequences and theatrics.... This idea came forward. Whilst Led Zepplin's original is the absolute business... My good friends' Tim, Del, Joe and Mark had recorded a cover of the track[11] with their Band. Mark was sadly killed in a motorcycling accident - and what better way for me, to pay tribute to my mate, than having him play drums at the start of the iconic ARC 100.

There are so many hidden stories in this race, and the more you learn the more poignant various places become.

I double checked my watch was all setup and ready to go as the countdown started from 10.

Three… Two… One… and we're off!

---

[11] You can find the cover at https://soundcloud.com/bare-knuckle-blues-band/kashmir

CHAPTER 6
Coverack to Porthleven

Friday 28th January 2022, 12:00pm

Start - 0 miles

Competitors Starting: **246**

This was it. Arc attempt number 4. I had my rule: I could stop if (a) I finished, (b) I got timed out or (c) I died. And I had a set of target times on my watch for a 34.5-hour finish, which I hoped to stay ahead of, but would also give me a bit of leeway if I fell behind. I was set. I was ready. And now, I was setting off on a 166-million-millimetre adventure.

At the front, people ran down the road and a few seconds later I was off in the crowd, heading down towards the seafront on the road, blue smoke filling the air from both sides as people held smoke grenades high above their heads. Sounds mad, but take a look at the start photos and videos online - it's quite an epic visual show as runners emerge from the smoke down to the shoreline.

Through the village, and then heading to the right I hit my first little queue as everyone squeezes through a narrow gap onto the coast path. This is one of the very few places on the course where it doesn't follow the South West Coast Path (which actually heads down to Dolor Point and then curves back inland). A little further on, a few speedy looking runners came in from the left, having gone the wrong way, added an extra hill and lost a whole load of places - it's so easy to muck up on this course!

The route carries on along a narrow, single-track path, the mud fairly firm but a little squelchy underfoot. There were a number of times over the next 10 minutes where everyone bunched up again, leading to quite a few stops and starts and making it difficult to get any sort of rhythm. Although, to be honest, the first 4 miles are surprisingly technical and difficult to get much of a flow even if you were out for a solo run.

The weather was grey, with an omnipresent mist/fog that just hung in the air. The Cornish have a term for this weather: *mizzle*. With the temperature at a balmy (for January) 11°C, the moisture in the air was good at keeping me cool as I ran. But it was also good at making everything wet – my glasses, clothes, and also the path.

The mud wasn't much of a problem for my Peregrine ST shoes as they are designed for mud, gripping well and giving me confidence (the ST in the name stands for "soft terrain"). But the path isn't just mud, there's a lot of rock as well. Given a coating of moisture from the air, a lot of those rocks might as well have been made of ice such was the grip of my shoes on them. This led to a lot of very cautious descents down steps and slopes, and a lot more tensing of ankles and legs than I'd have liked, especially this early on in the race. I also seemed to be making close acquaintance with way too many brambles and gorse bushes to stabilise myself and my fingers were starting to resemble pincushions. My poles would have been useful here despite my plan to start using them only from Porthleven, but they were impossible to get without stopping and taking off my pack, and there was nowhere to pull over on this narrow path. Besides, this early in a race, I was of the mind to just keep moving and make progress whatever the situation, so there was no way I wanted to stop.

After a while, the path opened and there was more opportunity to run at my own pace without pressure from behind or hold ups in front. I took the opportunity to have a look at my planned timings on the UltraTimes data field on my watch. But as I switched it on, it just told me that the race was due to start at 12:00pm on Friday. It hadn't got the memo that it was actually about 12:20pm on Friday. I had given it a test before the race as always and it worked, but obviously something was broken today. The options were: (a) throw my toys out the pram and quit, (b) find a laptop, edit the code and fix it, or (c) ignore it. I opted for the latter pretty quickly and with a surprising lack of fuss for me. What did it matter anyway? I was just going to run how I felt and see what happened.

Carrick - 3.7 miles		
2018	13:07	
2019	12:53	
2020	12:53	
2022	12:56	Target: 12:57 (1 minute ahead)

Competitors Remaining: **245**

(I've put tables like this throughout the book. They show the official GPX distance into the race at each point, along with the times for my various attempts. I've also included the number of competitors still in the race at this point, determined from the tracking data.)

At 12:56pm, I got to the first tracker point 3.7 miles in and just north of the islet of Carrick Luz, which was pretty much exactly the time I'd been aiming for. It's a tough, technical section, and I knew it eased off a little between here and The Lizard at about 10 miles in, before becoming generally more runnable terrain, at least for a while.

A little over a mile after Carrick, I went through the car park at Kennack Sands. It was a busy area, with all competitors still pretty tightly grouped after just 5 miles of racing, cheering and clapping crew members raising the spirits as we turned onto the road uphill and away from the beach car park. The hard, flat road surface was a short but welcome break from the muddy trails so far, and I took the opportunity to open up my stride a bit and power up the hill until we turned back onto the trail on the left.

Five minutes further along the route, we passed the old Serpentine works in the Poltesco Valley, now owned by the National Trust. When pilchard fishing dried up during the 19th century, the industry in the valley turned to making use of the unusual geology of the Lizard area. The key component was Serpentine, a rare rock nationally, but one that was common in this area and when polished rivalled marble for its beauty. After Queen Victoria visited Penzance in 1846 and ordered several serpentine ornaments for her house on the Isle of Wight, the local serpentine business became a boom industry. Using a water wheel initially, and then a steam engine, the works were used to prepare and polish the mineral for jewellery. The remnants of the chimney and building are visible from the path.

The name *Serpentine* comes from the Latin *serpentinus,* meaning "serpent rock". Considering the area of Cornwall we were in – the Lizard Peninsula - you'd be forgiven for thinking there was a relationship here, but the naming of the rocks and the area are purely coincidental. The Lizard Peninsula name is most likely a corruption of the Cornish *Lys Ardh* meaning 'high court', while the rock is named as it has a similarity to snake skin.

I was using the same tried-and-tested nutrition plan as the last few long races I've done. The plan was to have no carbs in the morning or for the first hour of the race, the theory being that it would make sure my body was in a fat-burning mood. From that point, I should then have some carbs to make sure the more energetic systems - needed for things like climbing steep hills - were fully fuelled. An hour had passed, so I tucked into half a Clif Bar.

Somewhere along this next section, I was chatting with a few people and someone asked my number so they could look me up on the tracker at the end of the race. I replied that it was number 206, "the number of bones in the human body. Unless you fall off the coast path", which got a laugh from a few people around. I can't take credit for the joke - it's what my dad said when I was chatting to him on the phone a couple of days before the race.

Along the coast path in Cornwall, there were various stiles to navigate over. I was more used to the typical (for Dorset at least) wooden stiles that you climb up onto and step over through a narrow gap, but in Cornwall they're far more diverse and interesting. Coffen stiles (from the Cornish *coffen* meaning 'man-made hole') consist of a granite slab laid horizontally across the path. And there are sheep stiles which are essentially a set of long granite pillars mounted through a stone wall, creating a set of diagonal steps up one side and down the other. All good fun early on, breaking up the running along undulating paths, but less fun later in the race when your legs are less fond of climbing!

More mud, more hills, more rock but progressing well, I dropped down into the harbour at Cadgwith 45 minutes later.

Cadgwith - 7 miles

2018	14:03	
2019	13:35	
2020	13:38	
2022	13:41	Target: 13:41 (on time)

Competitors Remaining: 245

In mediaeval times, Cadgwith (Cornish: *Porthkajnydh*, meaning 'cove of the thicket') was a collection of fish cellars in the sheltered valley, but from the 16th century people started inhabiting the village with pilchard fishing as the main occupation through to the 1950s. Houses and other buildings made from local cob walls with thatched roofs were built along the beach giving it the characteristic Cornish fishing village appearance. Fishing boomed here - in one 4 day stretch in 1904, almost 2 million pilchard were landed, with 1.3 million on a single day! Due to climate change and overfishing, pilchard is no longer economically viable, but the sea still yields crabs, lobsters, sharks, monkfish and conger eel which are sold both locally and abroad.

If you're a fan of Charles Dance films, then you might already know that Cadgwith was the setting for the 2004 film *Ladies in Lavender*, starring Judi Dench and Maggie Smith. And if you didn't, then you do now.

This was a good point for crew to meet their runners, and still being early on in the race there wasn't a lot of spread in the field so there were a lot of crew all in one place. The support this year was bigger and better than ever before: running past cheers, clapping and bells clanging, along with shouts of "well done!" can't help but motivate, bring a smile to your face and a spring to your step!

But only 7 miles in, I was definitely feeling the effects of the terrain, the mud and the slippery rocks. I knew this section was hard, so I wasn't too surprised, but it's still a bit worrying when you know you've got about 95 miles left to do and you're already tired.

But while having a conversation with myself in my head, I came to the conclusion that I was here to get the job done. I was here to finish. "It doesn't matter how you feel," was the phrase that started going round in my head. I feel tired - so what? I'm still going to put one foot in front of the other and keep going. So why worry about it? That logic seemed to work and stop me worrying, with "how I felt" just becoming another external thing that I had no real control over but wasn't going to stop me.

Less than 5 minutes along the path from Cadgwith is the Devil's Frying Pan. Once a big cave, the roof collapsed leaving a narrow archway at the entrance and a boulder-filled bay where the cave one stood. During rough weather, the water appears to "boil" in the bay and a large central boulder resembles an egg in a frying pan… typically Cornish!

In the distance, I could hear the fog horn of the Lizard lighthouse, and as I rounded a corner, I saw the top of the Lizard lifeboat station at Kilcobben Cove, with its funicular railway that carried the crew 45 metres down the cliff to the boathouse at the bottom. The Lizard is quite a big area, and the lifeboat station is almost 2 miles before the lighthouse who's horn I could hear in the distance. The race route goes around the lifeboat top station, down some steps and carries on along a very runnable path, the going getting considerably easier here than in the previous miles.

Another ¾ mile further on and I passed Wireless Cottage. Built in 1900 by Guglielmo Marconi, the building housed equipment used to receive wireless signals from the Isle of Wight, 180 miles away, proving for the first time that radio would work over the horizon, something which many scientists of the time thought was impossible. Marconi had a head for business and quickly commercialised the concept, turning the building into one of a dozen stations for ship-to-shore radio. It was the first coastal station to receive an SOS in 1910 when the *Minnehaha* ran aground off the Isle of Scilly and radioed for help.

The fog horn of the light house was getting much louder now, and for good reason considering the mizzle was making it impossible to see more than a few hundred metres. I counted the time between blasts at 30 seconds - one of those odd things to do while running along to pass the time. Soon I was running right in front of the big white building.

Built in 1752, it was composed of 2 towers with cottages in between, and was significantly upgraded in 1874 following a number of wrecks in the previous year. The visible, black compressed-air fog horns were installed in 1908 but decommissioned a little over 20 years ago, replaced with an electronic signal which gave one almighty blast as I was right in front of it! Rounding the corner, the next sounded surprisingly distant.

And almost immediately I was on the pathway to the car park at Lizard Point, with people clapping, ringing bells and shouting congratulations to all of us passing. The car park was busy with runners and crew, and an Arc support van – colloquially known as *Flying Angels* - was there so I took the opportunity to top up my water bottle. The time now was 2:31pm.

Lizard Point - 10.5 miles

2018	14:55	
2019	14:20	
2020	14:22	
2022	14:31	Target: 14:33 (2 minutes ahead)

Competitors Remaining: **244**

The South West Coast Path skims across the northern edge of the car park, with the most southerly point on the mainland UK a mere 250ft to the south. Heading out the car park and up a few steps by the Wave Crest Cafe, the path felt so much easier than those first miles. Running felt controlled, I was breathing easily and just keeping the effort at a very sustainable level. Miles were being ticked off, but I knew I wouldn't feel properly "into" the race until 30 or 40 miles.

Sometimes, your race just doesn't go to plan: there are DNFs, and then there are *Arc DNFs*. This was the case for Matt Gibson who had a nasty fall when he got to the Lizard. Luckily his crew were near, and he went off to hospital to get treatment, with the results shared on Facebook – a very wonky looking finger and some nasty gashes to his eye socket. Luckily, the finger was just dislocated and his eye socket wasn't fractured, and he's looking forward to coming back for a 3rd try at the Arc in 2023.

A couple of miles after Lizard, I went through the car park near Kynance Cove to another load of vocal support from crews. Here, the Arc route took another slight deviation from the official South West Coast Path, staying a little inland and joining back just around the north side of the cove.

Described as "one of the most beautiful stretches of coastline in the South West" by the BBC, this certainly isn't a bad area to be running along! The coarse grained, shiny, crystalline rock in the car park is primarily bastite, one of the two common serpentine minerals here. Just off shore, the islands and stacks are made of the other type – tremolite. Kynance is important to geologists because of this close proximity of the two types of the mineral in such a small area.

In the cove is the tidal Asparagus Island, named for the rare wild asparagus that can be found there. A fault eroded by the sea on the island has created a blow hole, and at about half-tide, a snorting sound can be heard - the sound of the *Devil's Bellows*.

I knew somewhere coming up was "the boggy bit" - a section of the path where you just couldn't avoid getting your feet soaked through. For my last 3 attempts at the Arc, the grass was mostly submerged under clear but cold water, with just clumps above the water level which I started hopping over, but eventually gave up and just squelched through the ankle-deep water until the end, my feet absolutely soaked. But a few weeks before the race this time, someone on the Arc Facebook group had pointed out that the official South West Coast Path actually goes *around* this boggy section, and I was hoping to put this new knowledge to the test and come out with dry feet.

Two miles after Kynance Cove, sure enough, the grass started to get soggy. I took a quick look over to the left and saw another path, so about-turned and started heading back to join it, much to the consternation of a few other runners. I shouted out that the official coast path is over there and it should avoid some boggy bits, but they were having none of it. I headed round anyway, a few minutes later glancing back to see some people were following. To my delight the whole ground was dry! It was maybe 100-150 metres longer, but I'd just saved my feet from a jolly good soaking and taken the "official" SWCP route too[12], the first time in 4 attempts... I did enjoy the smug moment!

As I re-joined the other route, I met a guy running at the same sort of pace as me. "How are you doing?" I asked.

"I'm a lot more fucked than I think I should be," was his reply. His name was Pip, and I liked him immediately!

---

[12] I did check on the Facebook group prior to doing this, and it was deemed that either route was acceptable for the race as there was almost no difference in length, although at the time the official GPX took the "wet" route.

We got chatting, and it turned out he had a decent history with ultras. He'd run Ultra Tour Monta Rosa (UTMR), a race I was a bit familiar with having holidayed in Saas-Fee in Switzerland a couple of times which is on the route. He's also done this race called... I forget... is it Ultra Tour Mont Blanc (UTMB)? Yeah, that's the one. Quite big, so I hear[13]! Although in our conversation, he did confirm something I'd heard in the past - that UTMR is more difficult than UTMB. But they're both very different to the Arc. Rather than continuous up and down on muddy trails, you get nicely groomed trails, but ascents can last 3 hours. Chatting to someone really passes the time, and the miles were ticking by now over what was pretty decent, undulating but not ridiculous terrain.

I was being a bit rubbish with my nutrition. I was supposed to be having about 40g of carbohydrates every hour (except for the first hour). As I finished the remains of my Clif bar somewhere around here, bringing my total to about 40g, I was conscious of the fact that I was nearly 4 hours into the race and I'd hardly eaten anything. I felt good though, but that's not a reliable indicator of how things are going to go as the race progresses, so I tried to make a conscious effort to eat more.

Just before 4pm we dropped down into Mullion Cove, a smidge over 17 miles completed.

---

[13] Just to clarify: UTMB is probably the biggest trail race in the world, with over 2,000 runners attempting the 106 miles and 33,000ft of elevation around the base of Europe's highest mountain within just under 2 days.

Mullion Cove – 17.2 miles

2018	16:37	
2019	15:53	
2020	15:46	
2022	15:52	*Target: 16:05* *(13 minutes ahead)*

Competitors Remaining: **244**

I remembered the place from 2020 when my insole had started sliding out the back of my shoe a mile or so before. Thankfully, I didn't need to do any impromptu cobblering this year, but I wanted to top up with some water and when a very friendly woman asked if I wanted anything, I asked her for some water. She looked totally confused at me, and at that point I realised she was actually talking to the runner she was crewing for who was just behind me! No bother, I knew there was a tap on the side of the building just as you re-join the path, so I stopped to top up. A couple of runners behind me clocked this and joined in with filling up bottles as I headed on up out of Mullion.

My toes were hurting now, and not in a way I was familiar with. The top of my toes seemed to be rubbing in my socks and the feeling was as if blisters were forming. I handled this in the usual way that I deal with a new niggle – to make a mental note of it, then ignore it and see if it's still bothering me in a few miles. Thankfully, on this occasion, whatever was causing the problem either stopped or disappeared into the background level of discomfort that grew throughout the race.

One and a half miles further on from Mullion, I passed a stone monument next to the path. Erected in 1937 by the Marconi company, this pillar commemorates the work of Marconi and his team of research experts and radio pioneers at the Poldhu Wireless Station between 1900 and 1935. The site was home to four huge 65m tall masts, and on 12th December 1901 Marconi sent a signal to Newfoundland, a distance of 2,100 miles. All that remains today apart from the commemorative pillar are the foundations of the 4 masts.

Shortly afterwards, the path joined a gentle downhill road to Poldhu beach. As I passed the beach cafe, I noticed a number plate on a white flat-bed truck that was very close to POLDHU - the closest I can recall was PO11 DHU, but looking that up suggests it's on a tractor which it certainly wasn't!

Over the narrow road bridge in Poldhu and back up the road on the other side we then slipped to the left, back onto the proper coast-path. The path continued in a pretty unremarkable manner, a trail cutting through grassland, undulating hills but nothing too memorable, not much mud, and nothing too slippery.

At Gunwalloe, just before 22 miles into the Arc, the long stretch of sand appeared below and to the left, stretching on to Loe Bar which was a key marker just a couple of miles from the first checkpoint at Porthleven. Still moving well and chatting with Pip, the route was passing by fairly innocuously, although the feeling that I shouldn't be quite as tired as I was at this point still nagged in the back of my head.

The sight ahead was quite beautiful. The fog/mist/mizzle had slowly cleared up since leaving Lizard, and a break in the clouds projected a beam of evening sunlight onto the buildings of Porthleven, just beyond Loe Bar. Sunset was in about 25 minutes, and the golden light brought a wonderful splash of colour to what had been a pretty grey day so far, while also highlighting our first rest point - if only momentarily - on the race.

A long event like the Arc can only be mentally processed if you break it into smaller chunks. Think about the remaining 80 miles to go, and your mind will (correctly) decide it's a bloody stupid idea and do everything it can to sabotage. Things will hurt more, risks will feel far scarier, the idea of sitting in a pub with a pint and not doing any more running will appear to be pretty much the most sensible idea you've ever had. So, you can't think about it like that - you have to look ahead to the next hill, the next cove, the next view. If you know the route, you can have some key points - the lighthouse at the Lizard, the boggy bit afterwards etc. While you try not to think too far ahead, the checkpoints are obvious big divisions of the route, and I genuinely didn't really think beyond the next checkpoint for most of the race. For me, right now, Porthleven - just a few miles away - was the end of my current perception of what I was doing.

The next couple of miles to Loe Bar were undulating but generally downhill, and on decent terrain, so it was just a case of getting on with it. The final descent passed close to the tall white cross of the monument to *HMS Anson*, erected in 1949. The memorial remembers the 1807 disaster where a naval frigate went down yards from the beach and more than 120 men lost their lives. The bodies were buried on the beach and cliffs; only a year later an Act of Parliament was passed requiring a proper Christian burial. A young man named Henry Trengrouse witnessed the horror of the shipwreck and went on to invent the *Breeches Buoy* - a sort of zip-line/flotation hybrid - that saved countless lives since.

At the bottom of the hill, the terrain immediately changed from hard-packed path to a wide stretch of coarse, flinty sand, covering just under 500m across Loe Bar - a sand bank with the sea to the left, and the largest freshwater lake in Cornwall to the right. Geomorphologists believe the Bar was most likely formed by rising sea levels after the last ice age, blocking the river and creating a barrier beach. Occasionally, the Bar has been intentionally breached to prevent flooding of parts of the inland town of Helston. The last time this occurred was in 1984, and the Bar has always resealed itself after human intervention.

As I dropped onto the sand, I kept running, but within 20 or 30 seconds I realised I was the only one still doing so and stopped to walk with everyone else. It quickly became apparent that walking - at least to me - felt harder. With running, I seemed to naturally end up on my toes and almost bounce across the sand before it sank, but when walking it felt like big steps were needed. I got back to running - slowly - and bounced my way all the way to the end overtaking quite a few people. It turns out Pip, just

84

behind me, was inspired by my fairy-prancing across the Bar and joined in as well.

It's worth mentioning my gaiters here. I had some pretty lightweight Montane Via gaiters which I've had for a few years and used a lot. When you use something and don't encounter any problems, it's difficult to know whether they're useful or not, but over the years I've had a few experiences with these gaiters that suggest they are an absolute lifesaver (if your life were to be ended by getting random little stones in your shoes at least). The ones I use have a plastic clip to attach to laces, or ideally a hook on the front of the shoe. This works perfectly with Altra shoes, but I had to snip away with a pair of wire cutters to get them to clip onto my Saucony shoes, and even then, they were an utter bitch to get on and off - something which I didn't appreciate later at Land's End! Once clipped onto the front of the shoe, they velcro at the back just above the heel. Again, Altra solve this with a built-in velcro strip, but for my Saucony Peregrines I had to superglue a sticky velcro patch onto each shoe.

Back in September, whilst wandering a chunk of the South West Coast Path at a leisurely 30 miles a day, the path met the beautiful, golden sands of Croyde Beach. My heart sank, and I assumed that not only would I have to trudge across a load of soft sand, but I'd also have to stop and empty my shoes. Half a mile later, I had not a single grain of sand in my shoes. And that has been the story every time I've used those gaiters. I'd highly recommend them… in fact, I'd go as far as to suggest sticking a pair on for every important trail run you do. With the velcro glued to the back of your chosen shoes, it only adds seconds at the start of a run, but saves the minutes to empty shoes, or potentially hours of bloody irritating sand and stones in your shoes while you decide whether to stop or not!

Now, where was I…? Ah yes…

With Loe Bar done, I was pretty much at Porthleven… or so I thought. That rose-tinted, heavily abridged memory thing you get in ultras can be a bugger. The path went up, round a sharp corner and up some more. Then up a bit more, with a few more zig-zags, and before I knew it, I'd climbed 100ft in ¼ mile, which isn't huge unless you sort-of remembered it being pretty much flat. Still, I was now on a tarmac path that undulated a bit, then dropped down to a car park and I ran along a stretch of road towards the town.

As the road hits the harbour and bears right, I passed the recognisable sight of the Bickford-Smith institute building with its 21-metre-high clock tower; a photo of this building with a huge breaking wave behind sometimes appears in the background of BBC weather forecasts, especially if wind and rough seas are forecast. The road narrowed, covered a short section of cobbles with a very old looking wall to the right and the water of the harbour to the left, then returned to standard tarmac for the last section to the end of the harbour, where I was met by Arc Angels who directed me along to the aid station.

Unlike my previous 3 Arc attempts, the Porthleven aid station was now in the football club, a new venue that I was unfamiliar with, cunningly hidden a good half mile away from the centre of the village. Up the road I went with Pip, passing - and congratulating - runners who'd done their CP1 maintenance and were off to face the next section. We were eventually picked up by an Arc Valet, another unique feature of this race. Close to the aid stations, the Arc Valets wait to meet and guide runners the last minute or two. Not only does this take away the issues with finding the right entrance to the buildings, but they can also check if you need anything while you're moving along and pass this info over to the checkpoint crew as you enter. It's a little thing, but a great help, especially later in the race. We followed a slightly convoluted route around a few corners, and moments later we headed into the main checkpoint building.

Porthleven (Checkpoint 1) – 24.4 miles

2018*	18:59 – 19:15	
2019	17:38 – 17:48	
2020	17:18 – 17:30	
2022	17:24 – 17:42	*Target: 17:51 (27 minutes ahead)*

Competitors Remaining: 243

(* 2018 included a very muddy 2-mile detour just before Porthleven)

First 3 and last 3 people who completed the race:

	Race Time	Time of Day
Mark Darbyshire	03:51:30	Fri 15:51:40
Dave Phillips	03:52:35	Fri 15:52:45
Tristan Stephenson	03:57:42	Fri 15:57:52
Tarne Westcott	06:14:42	Fri 18:14:52
Jason Mitchell	06:15:18	Fri 18:15:28
Simon Finn	06:26:27	Fri 18:26:37

At 5:24pm, I was at Porthleven checkpoint, having covered 25.2 miles just as the sun gave up lighting the sky and very sensibly went to bed. The official GPX route has the distance at 24.4 miles, so as is expected in ultramarathons, I'd already found an extra mile somewhere.

You've run a pretty tough 25 miles in a bit under 5-and-a-half hours, and you get offered food - what would *you* have? I already knew what was on offer, and ordered sausage and chips. And a cup of coffee.

Coffee. Caffeine. For the first time in 3 weeks. The first of my "secret weapons" was being deployed!

The people in the aid station at most ultrarunning events are great. The people in the aid stations on the Arc are fucking amazing! I'd barely walked through the door when I had 3 people asking what I wanted. My sausage and chips were ordered, a coffee was on its way and my soft flasks were off being filled up, half a pack of Tailwind being stuck in one of them. And I was one of 10... 15... maybe 20 runners that were in the place at that time, everyone feeling like the whole building was working for them, busy sorting out whatever they needed.

While the food and drink was coming, I took off my pack and took a seat. The first few ultras I did, I spent a long time in the aid stations, but you quickly realise that the faster you can be - within limits - the better. I say "within limits", because I've also made mistakes by being too quick, which have cost me later in the race. You need to be sensible. Don't sit down, put your feet up and watch the TV, but also don't charge in and charge out in 15 seconds flat as you're bound to forget something important.

In the back of my pack was the big bag of food which I needed at every single aid station. In Russian Doll style, it contained more bags of food, each intended for the sections between checkpoints, so at each stop I could quickly transfer it to the easily accessible front pocket. As I needed this at every checkpoint, I wrote myself some notes of the other things I needed to do and put it into the outer bag, so I'd be able to read it and remind myself of all the tasks at each and every checkpoint. Brilliant, huh? Yeah. I completely ignored it at every, single, checkpoint! But it was a good idea… just on this occasion my brain was working enough each time to know what I needed to do.

And at Porthleven, I needed light. Out came my head torch. I have at least 7 different head torches, and I've used them all a lot. Here's a piece of advice for anyone doing an endurance event – *use your kit in training!* It's such an obvious thing, but so many people I speak to while running along don't know how to use their watch, their race vest, their torch, their poles — all because they picked them up on the morning of the race and headed out with them, assuming it would be easy. When the kit doesn't work as expected, you've got no-one to blame but yourself!

A few years ago, I spotted a discounted Black Diamond Icon headtorch in Cotswold Outdoor and as I had a handy discount code, I bought it pretty much on a whim. It's probably not a well-known head torch, but I really like it because it has a big battery pack (4xAA batteries) that is detachable from the head strap. In the box, they supply an extension cable, meaning you can have a really lightweight head torch on your head, and a big battery pack on the end of a wire in your race vest. You get loads of battery life without having to lug a bloody great battery on the back of your head.

I also got out my little magnetic red flashing LED light which was part of the mandatory kit, and stuck it to the back of my race vest. Now the rules say you need to wear it for the whole race, but I didn't want the thing going flat in the middle of the night so I thought it better to put it on when I put my head torch on, here at Porthleven.

Before I had the chance to do anything else, my mini sausages, chips and coffee arrived, so I got on with the very important business of shoving things into my face.

This was also the point at which I'd planned to start using my poles. There was no particular terrain-related motivation for it, just that it was a good stop point and I'd have an opportunity to get the poles out without wasting any running time. I got out the

Salomon Pulse belt that I'd stuck into my back at the last minute (triggering my 10 minutes of panic back at Porthtowan trying to close the car boot!), and twanged it up my legs onto my hips. It was too tight but also very stretchy; I figured it might be useful and I was pretty sure I'd forget about how tight it felt soon.

I munched my way through the sausages, half the chips, lots of salt and finished the coffee. My soft-flasks had come back full up, and I tried to stick them into the race vest but didn't have much luck - I'm sure it used to be easier on previous Salomon vests, but with the current one it's just a pain in the arse trying to get them back into the stretch front pockets, especially if you're not wearing the vest at the time.

I'd drunk around 1.5 litres of water between the start and Porthleven, with the "emergency" half-litre stuffed in the back of my vest as yet untouched. And I'd had the coffee. But I was still thirsty, so I had another 2 cups of squash in the time it took me to get my vest on, get those damn soft flasks back in the front and stick my poles into the elasticated holders on the Pulse belt.

I'm going to take this opportunity to mention a vaguely relevant point. As I write this, being a "troubled author", I'm having a drink. Right now, it's a St Austell Tribute (despite being from Dorset, I'm a sucker for Cornish beer). I'm using writing as an excuse to murder my liver, and it's working quite well. But back to the (vaguely relevant) point - Skinner's Brewery in Cornwall makes a beer called Porthleven, and I've been rather enjoying it recently. The website says: "*Designed for modern palettes, our premium pale ale is a contemporary Cornish icon. Ask for a pint of this and receive an appreciative nod from St Ives to St Agnes, Perranporth to Porthleven itself!'* What a load of pretentious bollocks! But if you like a beer, then it does go down well.

A week or two after the race, I read a Facebook post about the Porthleven checkpoint, written by Emma Stephens, the manager of that aid station. It was a new venue which added to the complexity in organisation, but what they didn't expect was half the appliances to be broken - like the hob, when you have gallons of soup to cook! And to add to the fun, a whole bunch of the regular checkpoint volunteers were unavailable due to Covid. But as a runner coming through CP1, I had no idea about any of this. A testament to how the aid station crew just got on with it, worked around the issues and looked after the 250 runners coming through. Thank you everyone!

CHAPTER 7
Porthleven to Penzance

Stepping out the door of the Porthleven aid station at 5:43pm, Pip and I went entirely the wrong way. Thankfully, the checkpoint staff were used to idiots and sent us in the right direction, which was along a path, round a corner and to a dead end at a brick building.

We looked at each other and tried to come up with a sensible plan, this eventually involved actually opening our eyes and spotting the small arrow attached to the building, pointing around the back. We squeezed through into an area that both of us could only assume would be the sort of place you'd sneak for a quick piss out of sight, through some trees and found a well-hidden gate back out onto the pavement of the road we'd come up on. Ah, it's almost like someone actually had a plan for this route!

Roles swapped, we were now the people running along the pavement out of the aid station, passing people coming in the other direction on their way to get some fuel, drink and rest. Lots of "well done" and "keep going" swapped between us, then guided across the road by Arc Angels (presumably to make sure they didn't have to mop up any bits of tired runners that got splatted by cars) we were off up the road that led back onto the path proper.

I was running along with that Salmon Pulse belt on - the one I almost didn't bring with me. My poles were held around the back, and they weren't bouncing, they weren't rubbing, they weren't any kind of problem at all. They were immediately accessible, sat there innately, just waiting until I needed them. Thank you to the guy who mentioned the belt back at race HQ this morning - a brilliant, last minute kit addition!

I'm going off on a few tangents here, explaining things that are obvious to me but I'm not sure I've really mentioned before, so apologies but I hope it's useful or interesting and not too annoying. This one is about my navigation method, and it might be a few paragraphs as I do like a map and GPS…

Back in 2014, I bought myself a handheld GPS receiver - a Garmin eTrex 30 - which I've used for almost every single ultra since then (I didn't for Endure 24 as it's a 5-mile loop that's well signed, and even I'm not that bad at nav!). It's a little handheld jobby and takes 2 AA batteries so it's easy to carry spares, unlike devices with built in rechargeable batteries. Like my headtorch, I stick expensive, lightweight and very long lasting lithium batteries in which last about 25-30 hours. The eTrex has a trans-reflective screen, which means that unlike a mobile phone you can see the map in daylight without needing to use the backlight which is what makes the battery last so long. This applies at night too as you've got a head torch on, which is fine for seeing the screen. Through the Garmin website, you can download 1:25K OS Maps onto the device, so you get a fully detailed background map under your track and can see where you are - and what's around - at any point. There's the lowdown on the eTrex 30 - a great (if old) bit of kit. It's a bit slow when you zoom in, but other than that, it's small, light and the battery lasts for ages.

For my first Arc back in 2018, I was excited to be using my shiny new Garmin Fenix 5X, the first watch I'd ever had that had a base map, showing more than just your route. It was great to be able to navigate with my watch instead of holding the GPS, but 8 hours after starting with a fully charged battery, it was down to 10%. Luckily (or unluckily), I bowed out of that attempt not too much later so it didn't hamper me really. But it did sort-of scar me for using my watch for navigation, so from then on, I kept using my eTrex in my hand.

Bear with me... The problem with using a handheld GPS is that you can't really do it while using poles - it's one or the other. For the Arc in 2019 and 2020, I didn't use poles, partly because I wanted my GPS, but in both years, my knee caused me to DNF.

So, this year, poles were non-negotiable - my only real weapon against my unknown knee problem. I figured I'd done a good chunk of the Arc 2 or 3 times before, and even with my frankly worse-than-pathetic sense of direction, I'd be able to get myself along. But I'd have that trusty old eTrex easily accessibly in the front of my pack, and could grab it at any time if I was unsure of the route.

Finally, I'm going to get back to the point. As I left Porthleven, headed up the hill and back on to the path, I decided to start using my poles. And now, instead of having a Garmin Fenix 5X (with its 8 hours or so of mapping life), I had a Fenix 6X that - in theory - could last 20-30 hours even with the mapping active. I hit the appropriate buttons, brought up the route from Porthleven to Penzance and left my eTrex GPS tucked in the race vest. Long story short (short? Are you joking? Have you read the last 86 paragraphs about GPSs?!), it worked bloody well!

Out of Porthleven - following the trusty map on my watch while using my poles as well - I ran along the tracks leading around Trewavas Head and on to Rinsey. Just before Rinsey is the engine house of Wheal Prosper mine. Intended to mine tin and copper from the Porthcew Lode, it wasn't hugely successful, despite its name, working for only 6 years between 1860 and 1866. It's now a restored Grade II listed building, and quite a sight when it's suddenly looming out of the darkness. I have a big fascination and love of Cornish mining country, and catching sight of the building in my head torch as I ran past brought a big smile to my face. In a way, I felt like I was home.

I took the opportunity to try and be a bit better with my nutrition, got out my dog-poo bag[14] full of food and rifled around for a Nakd bar. Normally, I like these. Well, technically, normally I don't eat them as they're full of sugar and carbohydrates, but when I do, I like them. But not today. I had a bite, and it took a long while of chewing before I reluctantly swallowed. Within a few minutes, I was feeling a little dizzy in the head and sick in the stomach, a fairly familiar response to too much sugar in one go when I'm in the middle of an ultra. Not ideal, but I knew I just had to slow down a bit, not eat for a while and it should pass. It was making the running less comfortable, so Pip headed off as he was feeling stronger and able to maintain a better pace.

A mile or so later, I passed by a memorial at the spot where a stricken Sunderland Flying Boat crash landed on 2nd June 1943. While on patrol over the Bay of Biscay, the plane came under attack from 8 German aircraft. One crew member was killed, and the plane sustained heavy damage, yet after shooting down 3 of the German planes, the pilot managed to coax the aircraft back 300 miles before crash landing at Praa Sands, with the remaining 10 crewmen surviving. The memorial is a lovely carved stone piece, although I had absolutely no idea that I'd passed it as it was pitch black at the time. A minute later, I entered the car park at the northern end of Praa Sands Beach, pinging the tracker at 6:58pm.

---

[14] Yes, really… they're tough, cheap, brightly coloured so easy to spot if you drop one, and there's a box of them at home!

Praa Sands – 29.6 miles

2018	**20:50**	
2019	**18:59**	
2020	**18:41**	
2022	**18:58**	*Target: 19:48* *(50 minutes ahead)*

Competitors Remaining: 232

Now, I had a GPS and a watch showing maps and the route, both easily accessible. And I'd been here before, so I knew to turn left down towards the beach. But when some bloke in a van told me everyone is going right, I just ignored my instincts and a few hundred quid's worth of satellite-based navigation equipment and blindly turn right. I felt a little self-conscious 30 seconds later running quietly back past him in the correct direction towards the sea, then along the pathway by the railings that I remembered from previous years.

What I didn't remember is the load of water flowing down to the sea, mostly covering a set of slippery rocks that I had to cross. I would have reconsidered the route if it wasn't for the fact that some guy told me to "take it easy on the rocks" as I came down onto the beach, suggesting this was, in fact, the right way. I tiptoed across, getting more unsure of the direction despite the route on my watch confirming I was going the right way, then on the other side I headed right up to the road and found an entry to the coast path on the left-hand side.

Watching a video race report by *Ultra Runner Adam* on YouTube, he noticed the same issue. He'd gone the correct way, along the beach and across the water on the stones, but while getting some nutrition in with his crew and chatting to the camera, he was being passed by runners who'd taken the road way round. One to watch out for - from the car park at Praa Sands, make sure you take the *left* towards the beach, and don't go round the back on the road!

My stomach was back together after the Nakd bar issue earlier, so I wasn't feeling sick while moving now. But I was a bit disappointed with the effect of the coffee. I'd been caffeine-free for 3 weeks prior to the race, and my recollection of previous times I'd done this was of a massive boost, even with a little cup of instant coffee. But I didn't feel like I was getting any of that this time, although in reality it was probably perking me up a bit. On reflection, I think my fairly poor sleep for the week or so before the Arc this time round made me a bit more tired than usual, and there is only so much magic that caffeine can do.

When running in the dark, it's difficult to differentiate between one point and any other unless there's something very specific about the place, so the details around this area are somewhat hazy. I know the route went past Kenneggy Sands and Prussia Cove, and then came into Perranuthnoe at a small road crossing where I was met with clapping and encouragement. I topped up my water bottle again from the Flying Angel van and headed over the road back onto the path.

After the road crossing at Perranuthnoe, the path continues round Maen-du Point (Cornish for 'Black Stone', which immediately makes me think of John Buchan's *The Thirty-Nine Steps*), and along in the dark but with a glow in the sky from the bright lights of Penzance. A little further along I made a mistake I don't think I made in the previous 3 attempts. In 2018, just as I got to a point where you had to carefully take a slight right turn on the path, my head torch battery ran out and I was immediately plunged into darkness. That was the end of my relationship with the SupraBeam V3 head torch, although to be fair, it did come back on when I pressed the button, although I'm not sure that switching off without any notice is a great design choice to indicate low battery. The point of this little detour in my 2022 story is that this time, unlike every other time I ran the Arc, I incorrectly carried on straight past this slight right and headed down towards the beach at Trenow Cove, despite being warned against doing so in most of the race literature.

Thankfully it wasn't long before I had one of those sixth-sense moments that something wasn't right, checked my watch, yelled a few swear words and headed back up the hill I'd just come down - one unwritten rule of ultras: if you make a mistake, it's *always* uphill to correct it.

Now running back along the right path, I could hear loud, happy and possibly slightly drunken singing coming from the beach - it sounded like a bunch of girls having a rowdy but fun time down by the water. I know how much racket my teenage daughter and her mates can make after a pink gin or two!

The path headed slightly uphill, turned to the right and continued up a little more until at the top in the distance I could see streetlights and people waiting. A bell clanged and I was clapped as I popped off the dark path and into the lights of Turnpike Road in Marazion at just before half past eight.

Marazion – 35.8 miles

2018	23:03	
2019	20:31	
2020	20:13	
2022	20:26	*Target: 21:33* *(1 hour 7 minutes ahead)*

Competitors Remaining: 227

This was the start of a 7-or-so mile section of road, a complete terrain change from hilly, muddy paths. Mentally, it's a nice waypoint ticked off, and the change of feel, an opportunity - in theory - to up pace a bit and make the most of the good ground. I glanced at my watch and was surprised to see it was under 4 miles to the checkpoint, this was great news as I expected it to be further.

Crossing the road onto the pavement, I turned left and started running at a very gentle pace with stiff, aching legs, my poles clicking gently on the ground. On the left side of the road was a line of cars all the way down the road, several with boots open and runners and crew busily eating, changing shoes and filling packs.

I switched off my head torch as there was no real need for it and I could conserve the battery, the light from the street lamps being plenty to see the pavement ahead. Another runner was stiffly half walking, half running down the road and I said a quick hello as I passed him. Don't be under any illusion that I was effortlessly gliding by though; I was inelegantly shuffling along at about 10-minute miles with a determination to get the next few miles done and get to the checkpoint.

The poles were getting annoying at this point, the constant clicking on the ground and the lack of ability to just relax my arms, so despite what Stephen Cousins had suggested about using them on this section earlier that morning, I unclipped them from the gloves they attach to, folded them and tucked them into the Pulse belt. I'm so glad I wore that thing - it was so nice to easily put the poles away and for them not to be a bother, knowing that I could have them back out and useful in 20 seconds.

A mile or so later I'd passed by a bit more life in Marazion, a few people walking along the street, pubs and shops with some feeling of life. I glanced again at my watch to see how far I had to go, and was surprised to see it was a little over 4 miles - how could that be when about a mile before I had *less* than 4 miles? I got my GPS unit out and double checked, but sure enough, the distance was correct. I still have no idea where I got the "less than 4 miles" from when I came off the path into Marazion, but

I had to accept that I'd made a mistake and my journey to the checkpoint had now just jumped up by another 15 minutes.

This sort of thought used to really throw me, make me angry or upset, mess up my rhythm or just send me into a spiral of gloom. But I've had enough experience of these long events to know stuff like this happens. And it really doesn't matter. The checkpoint always was in the same place, no matter where I expected it to be. I'd get there when I got there, and this time of doing the Arc, the time was irrelevant – just finishing was the goal. Another mile of road was another mile of quicker progress compared to muddy trail, so I just accepted it and carried on.

Following the track on my watch screen, I took a left from the road I was on, then through a car park. Had it been light at this point, I would have been able to look to my left and see the impressive tidal island of St Michael's Mount right there. But it was pitch black, and I couldn't. For the fourth time in 5 years, I ran past it with no clue of what was just across the water.

Underfoot, the path got a little sandier but still firm enough to run on. I went through another car park, then into some dunes at the back and across a small bridge. Here I was faced with 2 options - to the left were more sand dunes and a route I didn't know, or to the right was a road with a pavement which I'd taken in previous years. I opted for what I knew, hopped down off the wall and ran the 200m or so along the pitch-black road. A van went past, beeping a couple of times which I took to be crew giving encouragement (might as well look on the positive side!), and then I headed left through a gap and back onto the path. A minute later, I went through yet another small car park and then joined the concrete promenade that I knew ran for what felt like a very, very long way all the way to Penzance.

My pace had dropped from about 10-minute miles when joining the road at Marazion to about 12 minutes per mile here a couple of miles later, and it didn't feel very comfortable at all. I do a lot of walking as part of my training and can walk quickly, so I decided to switch over and see how it felt. Immediately, I felt so much better! I quickly realised too that this would be a lot less impact on my knees - especially as I was on a solid concrete path - which may help in holding off my recurring knee issue that had plagued the previous 2 attempts at the Arc.

I was comfortably walking at 14 minutes per mile, and with a little less than 3 miles to go to the checkpoint at Penzance I had about 40 minutes remaining. A train went past to my right at quite a speed, a clear indication that the end of the line was still a fair way ahead. The bright lights of the train maintenance works glowed a few hundred metres away, while the lights on the curve of Mount's Bay all the way to Penlee Point on the far side of Penzance twinkled, highlighting the path I was to take over the next hour or so.

The running had felt like hard work, but I was actually really enjoying walking. I felt relaxed, like I was floating along, and my legs and knees were benefiting from the different muscle and joint use. I didn't have any music on yet - that was coming soon - but I've got a decent memory for songs so started up the music player in my head. I picked *Sultans of Swing* by Dire Straits - the live version from Alchemy, over 10 minutes long and full of drum and guitar solos! I couldn't have cared less what anyone else thought as I speed-walked along the Penzance promenade, air-guitaring, air-drumming and badly singing Mark Knopfler's lyrics - I was having a blast!

The field was fairly spread out by now. I could see a flashing red light in the far distance, and behind was a single head torch, slowly gaining on me. As the runner caught up with me, he stopped running and we walked along chatting for a few seconds, at which point he said he couldn't keep up with my walking pace and got back to running, heading slowly off into the distance.

I'm not quite sure where the boundary of Penzance is, but as I walked the long promenade beside the train tracks, I surely passed some arbitrary point where Marazion became "central Penzance", the most westerly major town in Cornwall, and the base for Gilbert & Sullivan's comic opera *The Pirates of Penzance*, which I was (un)lucky enough to have had to study in English at school! The name Penzance comes from the Cornish *Pennsans*, meaning 'holy headland', and refers to the location of St Anthony's chapel that stood on a headland to the west of the harbour. And your final Penzance fact for today: it was the birthplace of the chemist Sir Humphrey Davy (chemistry is more my thing than English, so I like this one): he discovered electrolysis, isolated sodium for the first time, discovered nitrous oxide (what a laugh![15]) and possibly most importantly invented

---

[15] Nitrous oxide is used for sedation and pain relief, and commonly called "laughing gas". Apologies for my bad science joke.

the Miner's Safety Lamp (aka Davy Lamp), which stopped people blowing themselves up down the mines. Bit of a legend, was Sir Humphrey.

After what didn't feel like too long at all - another one of those expectation-vs-reality moments, as I remembered the trek down the railway taking what felt like approximately 2 weeks in the past - I was passing Penzance railway station, then heading through (another) car park, over a road bridge and past the Penzance ferry terminal. A left turn by the Jubilee Pool (one of the oldest surviving Art Deco swimming baths in the country), and I was on a widening promenade with some twinkling head torches in the far distance. The Arc Angels were there to guide the runners across the main road, but it wasn't busy and I was straight across, walking with an Arc Valet up to the rugby club where the second checkpoint was located and through the doors at 9:18pm.

Penzance (Checkpoint 2) – 40 miles

*2018**	**23:52**	
*2019**	**21:01 – 21:16**	
2020	**20:59 – 21:17**	
2022	**21:18 – 21:35**	*Target: 22:30* *(1 hour 12 minutes ahead)*

Competitors Remaining: **225**

(2018 and 2019 checkpoint was in a different location, approximately 1 mile short of the current location)*

First 3 and last 3 people who completed the race:

	Race Time	Time of Day
Mark Darbyshire	06:22:11	Fri 18:22:21
Dave Phillips	06:29:08	Fri 18:29:18
Tristan Stephenson	06:29:17	Fri 18:29:27
Iain Walker	10:34:43	Fri 22:34:53
Simon Finn	10:41:45	Fri 22:41:55
Dylan Gould	10:43:27	Fri 22:43:37

I was glad to be stopping, but didn't want to hang around too long. There were a lot of seats but they all looked busy with people or kit spread out, so I stiffly knelt down on the floor near the door and fiddled around in my bag. Like at Porthleven, the checkpoint crew couldn't have been more helpful. With my collapsible cup extracted from my pack, a coffee was on its way and my water bottles were being filled. I looked around at the food and quickly settled on a few slices of pepperoni pizza. You'd think that sort of food might not be great sat in your stomach when you're out running (or walking fast at least) again in a few minutes, but I didn't have a single problem with "real" food during this whole event.

I sorted my on-the-go nutrition out, bringing a few things from the back of my pack and swapping them to the front. It was pretty clear I'd been very bad at eating anything. I should have been piling through the various bars and snacks that I had with me and be disposing of masses of empty wrappers by now, but I was eating almost nothing and I knew this wasn't great. I was rapidly hating the idea of anything sweet, so I reorganised my food to put more savoury snacks in the front - nuts, Pepperami etc - and dumped a few of the sweeter things in the back. I made a note to myself – again – to at least *try* and eat more. It wasn't that I was feeling sick, I just wasn't feeling hungry out on the run and was concentrating too much on making progress, or on navigation, and pretty much just forgetting to eat. Easy to do, a simple mistake... and potentially a DNF waiting to happen.

Forty miles in the bank, 9 o'clock at night, it was time to break out parts 2 and 3 of my secret weapon - my legal performance enhancing drugs, if you will. The first part, as I mentioned, was having 3 weeks off caffeine and then having coffee at each checkpoint.

The second part was music. I deliberately waited a good chunk of the race so I had something to look forward to, and I'd get a decent psychological benefit. I dug my MP3 player and headphones out from the drybag in my pack. I take a separate MP3 player (well, actually, 2 of them, so I've got a backup) as my phone battery is pretty rubbish when it's on and I'm fairly sure I wouldn't even get 10 hours out of it. This cheap little MP3 player has an 85-hour battery life, and I stick it in a plastic freezer bag to keep it protected from rain and shove it in the front of my pack. It's full of about 100 albums I may listen to, so lots of choice, and I stick just one wired earphone in so I can still hear everything that's going on around me while having background music to listen to. I use the left earphone, as on this course the sea – and therefore the interesting weather – is usually from that side, and having something in your ear can be useful for protecting it from hours of wind.

Back in 2019, when I had that "best race ever" experience, the music I had on was Bring Me the Horizon's *Amo* album, so that's what I put on today. I deliberately hadn't listened to it for a long time, so it was fresh and would hopefully bring back some of that 2019 magic to tonight's running.

The third part of my secret weapon was paracetamol. After 9 hours and 40 miles of moving, everything hurts. Nothing too serious, but knees ache, ankles hurt and muscles moan. Something to take the edge off that lot can only be a good thing.

One important thing to note: I *never* take ibuprofen during an ultra - it's a very bad idea. Ibuprofen (and I believe other non-steroidal anti-inflammatory drugs or NSAIDs) decreases blood flow to the kidneys and during an ultra-endurance event, combined with dehydration and increased effort, this can cause serious problems. I know of one competitor who took 6 ibuprofen tablets during the Thames Path 100 and ended up in hospital for 2 weeks afterwards with serious kidney issues. I'd strongly advise staying away from ibuprofen during an ultra!

But paracetamol doesn't have this issue, so with my coffee I popped a couple, along with another slice of pizza, and some watermelon. On the big table at the aid station, I also noticed some bags of crisps and wrapped brioche rolls, so grabbed one of each to stuff into my pack.

17 minutes after entering Penzance checkpoint, now with a belly full of pizza, coffee and paracetamol and Ollie Sykes shouting *Mantra* into my ear via a headphone, I was heading back out with a mix of excitement and trepidation at what was coming. Shit was about to get real!

CHAPTER 8

Penzance to Land's End

Out of the checkpoint, it was a case of retracing steps down to the main road, safely crossing and then turning right at the seafront and heading west.

I stuck with walking rather than running as the next few miles were still on the road, but the caffeine had obviously worked this time as the first two miles were covered in just over 25 minutes, a decent walking pace by most standards! The route took me to Newlyn, not only the largest fishing port in England, but also the location of the *Ordnance Datum*.

How do those chaps and chapesses at the Ordnance Survey know how high to mark a contour on an OS Map? Well, at the Newlyn Tidal Observatory, over a period of 6 years between 1915 and 1921, they measured the tide height every 15 minutes (over 210,000 readings!), averaged them and used that as the "zero" point for all contour lines in the whole of the UK.

The tidal observatory building houses a brass bolt whose head is at exactly zero metres. It is situated in the Newlyn Tidal Observatory building next to the lighthouse on the end of the South Pier in Penzance harbour, which - slightly irritatingly for this story - I had passed 40 minutes and one checkpoint before reaching the harbour at Newlyn.

The route took me down a narrow road and past a used-car garage with a polished but somewhat beaten-up silver Mazda MX-5 in the window for sale. Onto the main road through Newlyn, I passed the Swordfish Inn. Inside, a decent rock band were playing, and being almost 10pm on a Friday night, there were plenty of happy people outside the pub, vaping, smoking and trying to stand up straight. I got a few claps and people saying "well done" from those who obviously knew what we were up to, which is always nice. Everyone gets involved in this race! A little further on, a group of very, *very* drunk chaps of about 20 years old were staggering along the middle of the road, one of them almost tripping over the curb. I was expecting a comment or two as I passed at my unusual speed-walking pace, but I think they were all too drunk to notice.

Heading on to Cliff Road at the far end of the harbour, I began a gentle ascent up the hill on the pavement. My poles were unobtrusively held on my belt, everything else sat nicely in my pack, music in my ears and a general sense of contented enjoyment as I stormed my way along!

All along the road were parked cars. Every few cars was one with the boot open and runners sorting things out, or the engine purring quietly as the occupants stayed warm waited for their runner to come by.

At one point I thought I heard a guitar, and as I rounded the corner a guy was sitting in the back of his car, playing and singing.

I'm a bit of a fan of live music of any genre, there's just something great about people playing and singing, and this guy was very good. I gave him a clap as I passed and shouted a thank you to him. From reading Facebook comments after the race, he brightened a lot of people's mood with renditions of *Eye of the Tiger*, *Lovely Day* and *500 Miles*, popping up later in the race too, a few miles after Pendeen. Those few short seconds of hearing the music was a wonderful thing that left me smiling for the next mile or two.

Mostly smiling, anyway. Ahead on the left was a fence that I recognised. Just behind was the old Penlee Lifeboat station, now disused and quietly hiding a dark story from 40 years before.

Off this coast on 19th December 1981 during a ferocious storm, the mini-bulk carrier *Union Star* was stranded, storm water having flooded one engine. When it was clear that the 8 people on board were in serious trouble as the ship was being blown towards the rocks at Boscawen Cove, a Sea King helicopter from RNAS Culdrose flew over but they were unable to winch anyone from the ship as the wind was too violent.

At 8:12pm, the wooden 47-foot *Solomon Browne* lifeboat was launched from this very lifeboat station, with 8 volunteer crew on board, into 100mph hurricane force 12 winds and 18m high waves. Several attempts were made to come alongside the *Union Star*, and a radio message saying "We've got four off" came back to shore, at which point the hovering helicopter turned back to shore assuming the lifeboat would head back also.

But it made one more attempt. There was no more radio communication. And 10 minutes later, the lights of the lifeboat disappeared. The next day, the *Union Star* was found capsized on the rocks near Tater-du lighthouse, and wreckage of the lifeboat began to wash ashore.

16 people were lost that night. Fortunately, it was the last time the RNLI lost an entire crew in action.

Every year on 19 December, the Christmas lights at Mousehole are dimmed between 8 and 9pm in memory of those who lost their lives, leaving just an illuminated cross and pair of angels shining down across the village and out to sea.

As I passed, I stopped for a moment, and saluted. I've no idea whether RNLI people salute, but it felt appropriate to show respect in some way and that's what I came up with.

Mousehole – 42.7 miles

2018	**DNF**	
2019	**21:56**	
2020	**21:48**	
2022	**22:11**	*Target: 23:28*
		(1 hour 17 minutes ahead)

Competitors Remaining: **207**

I entered Mousehole without really realising until I got near the harbour which is quite recognisable, even at night. I've taken many different paths through the village in the past and I've never been quite sure what the correct route is, but the line on my watch map was clear and obvious so I just carried on my odd speed-walk, twisting left and right as a guy running behind me slowly caught up.

Since Marazion, the whole route had been on road and mostly flat, any hill was very gradual and almost unnoticeable. That changed as soon as I turned towards Raginnis Hill, which climbed about 200ft in half a mile... and really felt like it! It was steep, although it was also nice to be doing something other than flat road finally.

At the top of the hill, a couple of Arc Angels were waiting to guide people to the left of the road and onto the trail again to start the next section to Lamorna Cove, part of the course known to be particularly hard work. Bushes grew up both sides and I was back in head-torch territory.

The path in this section starts easily enough, it's just a dirt trail on a gradual descent. A few more puddles appear, some rocks in the middle of the path that you just step over, and a glimpse of the fairly thick trees above in the head torch light. As you carry on, the mud becomes a bit thicker, the rocks become a bit bigger, and the route becomes a bit more technical.

It's less than 2 miles from the start of the trail to Lamorna Cove, but it quickly feels like you're on a different path to anything else so far. And the miles feel longer here too – they certainly take longer! I remember Colin Bathe - who put together the GPX route and route description documents for the Arc -

describing this section as having things like "water features" to climb up and down, and he wasn't wrong. Along the path, you'd meet a set of steps that twisted and turned, partly covered in mud with flowing water down the rocks. Wide bits swapped with narrow, feet-trapping sections, and my poles saved me from going flying a few times on this section. Having said that, the poles did have a habit of getting caught in the undergrowth, and they felt a bit like they were slowing me down on the stepped descents, but the key point of using them was to save my knee so I kept then handy.

There was one particular section I was looking out for - a bit on the path where you enter a clearing and it's not obvious which direction to head in. I've met this part before in both daylight and night-time, and on all occasions ended up completely lost within an area that can't be much more than about 20 square metres! Last time I was there back in September, I got in a muddle again but when I extricated myself I made a note of the correct route so I wouldn't do it again. It turns out that all you have to do is keep going pretty much straight ahead, but as you hit the clearing the obvious route looks like it takes you to the right, and then you get trapped in a tree-branch filled pocket of woodland.

Anyway, today I got to this section, recognised it and immediately... went the correct way! Good in the sense that I didn't lose any time, and also good that it was another one of those random mental milestones that I could tick off.

More twisting and turning, more climbing and descending, the sea crashing into the rocks on the left side. At one point, I clouted my knee on a big rock while climbing over. It hurt quite a bit, but another odd thing in the middle very long runs is that pain like that is quite... nice. It's not pleasant in the sense that "yeah, I'd love to give my knee a good bash!", but more that because everything from my neck, shoulders and arms down through my back, hips and especially leg muscles and feet was hurting, a sudden, acute pain in my knee was all consuming and a single focus. I knew it wasn't anything serious and after a bit of customary swearing I just got on with moving as the pain became an ache and eventually disappeared altogether beneath the background of other painful bits.

Around a corner I saw lights in the distance: Lamorna Cove. I carried on, a bit more clambering over some big rocks and avoiding tripping over some little ones. If there was a cover shot for an imaginary video of my exhilarating 2019 race, it would be this point. I have a probably highly inaccurate, rose-tinted memory of skipping over rocks here with grace and elegance, singing along to music and grinning from ear to ear as I effortlessly glided across the difficult terrain.

Today, I wasn't having a bad time either. It wasn't effortless, and I certainly wasn't gliding, but I was enjoying the music, enjoying the flow and movement and generally having quite a lot of fun! Down the hill, through mud and puddles I headed, and out into Lamorna at just before 11pm.

The car park was so busy! As I previously mentioned, the race had a lot more participants than any other time I'd done it, and it really felt like it. Gone were the days of quietly popping up at some village and there being just an Arc Angel van. Now there were cars and people everywhere, even in the middle of the night. The support is brilliant, but part of the appeal to me of this race is the solitude of the night sections, and so far, those quiet, solo sections had been a bit few and far between. I was always swapping places with people, lights ahead and behind, and crew cars and vans every few miles.

I didn't see a Flying Angel van in the car park and wasn't in desperate need of water so just carried on to the right of the cove, past the cafe where in the past I'd had a very nice pasty and possibly the hottest coffee ever. Round the corner was a lone van, an Arc Angel greeting me as I approached. "How's it going?" he said.

"I'm having a lot of fun!" was my reply. And I was! But it felt a bit wrong to say it - like now that I'd said it out loud, it would all go wrong.

I topped up my water bottle given the opportunity was here. A blister had started forming on my right thumb from using the poles, not something that's happened with these Leki poles before. I asked if there was a plaster in the van somewhere and after much digging around, he finally found a first-generation Compeed from sometime last century and I tried to stick it to my sweaty, wet thumb. It didn't take well, but sort of hung on there and I thanked him and hoped it would stay put under the glove I was wearing for the poles.

I headed off towards the small but technical climb out of Lamorna, the Compeed lasting about 30 seconds before falling off. I tucked it into my vest to throw away at the next stop.

Before the first time I did the Arc back in 2018, I did a brief recce of a few areas of the course. I was in Cornwall for a half term holiday at the end of October, and somewhat annoyingly I'd had my appendix out about 3 weeks previously so was quite limited on how far I could explore. I remember the visit to Lamorna, walking around this corner and finding the rocks ahead. Because of my operation, I couldn't climb over the rocks, so it stuck with me as a sketchy section, with climbs and drops and unknown danger beyond. It became a focus of nervousness in the first race, so much so that it subconsciously became part of my excuse to DNF at Penzance that year.

Since then, having done it twice in the race and twice in the other direction in daylight, I love this section! Sure, it's a bit of clambering over rocks with a drop to the left high enough to mess you up if you fell off, but that's the point - it's technical, it's interesting, and it feels like you've accomplished something by getting up onto the path. And, like most of the rest of the path, you'd have to really try hard to actually fall off.

With all that experience, I obviously knew exactly which route to go and which rocks to climb. So, it was a bit of a surprise when I found it a little difficult getting up a sloped but sheer rock that was a bit big to easily clamber up... especially holding poles. I unclipped the poles from my gloves and tightly held on to them as letting go would have most likely sent them off the edge and down into the crashing sea below. Gripping the top and pulling hard up the rock, I balanced my way to the top. That was the point where another guy - who'd gone the *right* way - yelled down from a higher path that it was "easier up here!" Bugger. Still... I was committed now (I wasn't really... I could have gone back round, but instead I chose to carry on like an obstinate twit), clambered up a couple more rocks that were a bit big to be comfortably stretched up and got to the path. I feel most sorry for the guy behind me who wrongly assumed I wasn't an idiot.

The path didn't get easy at this point, just flatter. The rocks to avoid were quite big, and involved a lot of stepping through small gaps, twisting left and right, and using hands to manoeuvre. It was irritating, impossible to get into any rhythm and there was no running to be had, just careful walking. This lasted for no more than about half a mile - 10 minutes at most - but my mood changed from the fun I was having at Lamorna into a bit more of a gloomy concentration, having to work at moving rather than the miles just sliding past.

The mizzle was back, the air damp and the moisture reflecting in the head torch light. The arms of my base-layer glistened with droplets of moisture, and my feet were soaked. Usually, my double-sock system means that if I go through a puddle or a bit of wet ground, the outer Drymax sock gets a bit wet, and in the worst case I feel the water get through the second pair to my feet, but within 5 minutes or so on a dry bit of path everything is back to feeling dry. But here, on this path, there just wasn't 5 minutes of dry ground. The path itself was mostly wet, either as mud or water just running along the top. And where it wasn't, the undergrowth around was covered in moisture and soaked my shoes from above. Although I didn't notice at this point, the constant wetness of my feet was beginning to become a problem.

As the path settled down to be a little more sensible, I could see the beam of Tater-du lighthouse sweeping through the omnipresent mizzle out to sea. Switched on in July 1965, Tater-du is the newest lighthouse in Cornwall and was completely automated from the start. It was constructed after the *Juan Ferrer*, a small Spanish coaster, capsized on the 23rd of October 1963, tragically costing 11 lives. At the base of the cliffs here, the wreckage of the *Union Star* was found on the morning of the 20th of December 1981. Another sober moment of reflection as I made my way past.

Honestly, I was expecting this bit to be easier than it was. I don't really know why, as it was well known to be a demanding section of the course, but that difference between my expectation and reality was knocking my mood further and I was beginning to feel a bit shit. In a mile, I'd gone from quite enjoying myself to wondering what I was doing out here and starting to contemplate the totality of the remaining distance, which was a bad idea.

It was taking 20 minutes or more to cover a mile, with lots of up-and-down paths, and every few hundred metres some technical sections required clambering up or down rocky steps or skittering across stones and deep mud. At one point I misjudged the ground and ended up knee deep in mud, accompanied by much swearing into the Cornish night. I was meeting lots of people too, mostly from behind as they overtook me, suggesting I was going slower than I should be. Whether that's true or not I don't know, but it's difficult to stay positive when you keep getting overtaken, especially if you don't have a rigid plan that you can use as an excuse for going slowly.

It did become apparent after a while that I was moving better on the less technical sections than others. I'd get overtaken by one or two people and they'd disappear off into the night as we were clambering up or down some rocks, steps or slopes. But once the going got better and the path became flatter and easier, I'd soon catch them up and overtake again. I think in hindsight that my poles were really slowing me down on the technical sections where using hands and some confidence in my shoe grip would have let me move significantly quicker. But on the very big plus side, my knee wasn't even hinting at hurting so far, and if that was down to the poles then they were 110% worth using, even with the speed hit.

But one point where the poles were a bloody nuisance was St Loy's Cove, which I hit just before midnight. The path drops onto a beach of rocks, reminiscent of huge dinosaur eggs, that you have to traverse for about 120 metres. Back in September, with good grip on my shoes, dry weather and even with poles, I pretty much skipped my way across the boulders in no time at all. But now, with wet shoes and wet rocks, the poles did nothing but slip causing me to nearly fall a few times, almost breaking the poles at least once as they got jammed between the boulders. As

I was inching forward, super-cautiously testing every step, a guy went past quickly like he was walking on a flat path, making me feel a bit of an idiot. I decided to tuck the poles away and trust my feet, at which point my speed about trebled and I got to the end of the rocks and back onto the coast path.

I don't remember much of the terrain between St Loy's cove and the next significant place - Penberth - but it took 35 minutes to cover the 1.8 miles so it must have been typical tough Lamorna-to-Porthcurno terrain of steep climbs, narrow paths and odd stone features to climb.

Penberth – 49.1 miles		
2018	DNF	
2019	23:47	
2020	00:14	
2022	00:26	Target: 01:49 (1 hour 23 minutes ahead)

Competitors Remaining: **203**

Penberth is a beautiful fishing village during the day, but just a house or two caught in a head torch at night. Heading past the houses and slightly inland, I then had to cross the Penberth river which is done with the aid of a set of 11 chunky stepping stones to hop across. Literally 60 seconds after I entered the tiny village, I was back out again on a path heading up another hill. A glance at my watch showed it was now Saturday at just about 12:30am.

Not much more than a mile further on is Porthcurno, famous for being the place where the first transatlantic telegraph cables landed, and home of the Minack theatre. I still had that mile to do though, and although the path was less technical there was still a fair amount of uphill out of Penberth so I wasn't moving quickly. Just before Porthcurno I took a wrong turn - or rather didn't take the right (left) turn. Had I carried on, I would have ended up in the car park for the beach, somewhat confused and annoyed. As it happens, I realised pretty quickly due to the incessant checking of the map on my watch, did the customary swearing and about turned to go back up the hill and spot the (now) right hand turn down to the beach. Another runner was waiting at the top looking a bit unsure, so I helped out and we both went down the correct path to the beach and around the back on the sand. I looked out for the little white cable hut - the point where those thousands of miles of undersea cables actually came above ground - but couldn't see it from where I was, so carried on and took the path up towards the steps to the Minack Theatre.

At the bottom of the steps, a guy was looking in the grass for something that I presumed he must have dropped, although I couldn't quite figure out what you'd have dropped while running that would involve such a close inspection of the ground. As I passed, I realised he wasn't looking, but was in fact emptying the contents of his guts all over the ground! I checked he was OK, and he signalled that he just needed a moment, so I carried on. Funny old world, this ultrarunning malarkey. If you shifted most of what we see and do in the night after 12 or more hours of running to the daytime on a normal street, you'd either end up with an ambulance or the police being called!

Knowing about things like the steps at the Minack can make you a bit apprehensive about them, but there's no need really. Yes, they're hard work, for a minute or two. But so is 90% of the rest of the course - a lot of it harder. There's really nothing to concern yourself with. I remember feeling quite dizzy going up these steps in 2019 and having to stop half way up, but this time I took the steps one at a time, slowly but continuously and before I knew it, I was on the steep but flat path next to the fence at the very top. Bells rang from the top and cheers and clapping drifted down, another great welcome from crews even at 1am!

I looked around in the car park for the Arc Angels, spotted the most illuminated van and headed over. This time as well as topping up water, I got a cup full of coke. In previous years I'd managed to over-consume caffeine by this point and was getting shakes from too much, but this time round I was still feeling quite tired so figured an extra poke from the coke could only help.

The Minack is a key point on the Arc route. It's the midway point of the 100 (although I'd covered 51.7 miles at this point), and it's the start of the Arc 50. In 7-and-a-half hours time, another group of a couple of hundred runners would start off from here, covering the route that I was just beginning now.

It's a wonderful place to start a race too - an impressive stone amphitheatre set at the top of the cliff against the backdrop of the sea. In 1931, the site was a gorse-covered slope at the top of a 90-foot cliff. Following a successful open-air production of Shakespeare's *A Midsummer Night's Dream* by the local theatre group, the following year Rowena Cade offered the use of her cliff garden for the show. She set to work preparing an area for the audience to sit... and kept working at it all her life. The whole theatre was built by hand from rocks and using concrete mixed with sand from the beach that she carried up herself. Cade died in 1983, but the theatre lives on, with some 80,000 people a year seeing a show and more than 100,000 paying an entrance fee just to look around the site.

Readying myself to head off, a thought occurred to me. Last time I did the Arc, back in 2020, my knee was screwed by this point. The next 4.7 miles to Land's End took me hours of careful, slow movement, despite it not being particularly technical. And in 2019, it was somewhere over this next stage that my knee began to fail. So far, I wasn't getting any signals that concerned me... my knee hurt, but more on the front, the kneecap, rather than the inside of my leg as had been the problem before. And more importantly, the left knee hurt in the same way, implying this wasn't an injury with my right leg, but just two knees that were a bit knackered, having carried me over 50 miles!

Time to go. Through the car park and back into the darkness on a path cutting through grass with granite chunks underfoot. When I walked this section of the Coast Path in the other direction back in September, I wasn't having a great day between Land's End and Penzance. I remember it being pretty dull - fantastic cliff formations, but the path was undulating without much interest, wide open and not particularly exciting. But after the ups-and-downs, mud, water and technical aspects of the previous 5 or 6 miles, "dull" was perfect.

Somewhere around here I met up with Pip again. I don't remember exactly where, but I have a memory of a cheerful "hello again!" from someone in front, somewhere around a little bridge. I'm rubbish at recognising people's faces at the best of times, but when they've got a head torch strapped on and I can't make out any features at all I might as well give up. But his voice is distinctive, and we quickly settled back into easy conversation.

Pip was having stomach issues and struggling a bit. He was shuffling along, continuing to run and I didn't want to point out to him at this point that I was walking behind him at the same speed he was running. The terrain, as I remembered, was open and while continually undulating it wasn't tough, more reminiscent of the South Downs than a technical coast path trail. Moving at a reasonable pace was easily possible, but I was happy to be fast walking, occasionally running along while we chatted.

The miles from Minack to Land's End felt like they went by surprisingly quickly, I think down to the easy conversation with Pip. We switched between running and walking, taking in a few fairly sharp descents, bridges or stepping stones across waterways and up valleys.

We passed through Porthgwarra, a tiny village on the beach, and up onto Gwenapp Head, passing the National Coastwatch Institution (NCI) lookout station. The NCI was formed in 1994 following the deaths of two local fishermen who drowned below a recently closed lifeguard station at Bass Point on the Lizard Peninsula. In 2019, more than 2,600 uniformed, trained volunteer watchkeepers maintain a visual watch along parts of the UK coastline, with 54 established watch stations, reporting any emergencies to the appropriate authorities.

There were a few hills around here, and as we came over the top of them, the westerly wind was becoming a lot stronger and more noticeable. Whilst getting blown around on top of one hill, the bright lights of the Land's End hotel were clearly visible in the distance. Having done this a few times before, I told Pip what they were, but to not get too excited as its deceptive and takes bloody ages to get what seemed like quite a short distance. Sure enough, around Nanjizal about 20 minutes later, we went over the top of another hill and the lights looked pretty much exactly the same distance away.

There was one section of narrow path cut into a steep slope where I commented that you really wouldn't want to fall - it was a long way down to the left and the waves crashing loudly into the rocks suggested it wouldn't be a soft landing. Although I'd have to make a fairly catastrophic error to fall off the path, I still, slightly nervously, shuffled quickly along that section.

As was becoming a habit, the footsteps accumulated, the distance got covered and the trail turned to something more man-made as we passed Greeb farm and were met by Arc Valets to guide us up to the Land's End Hotel: checkpoint 3, over halfway, and the stop where you can get your drop bag.

Now I really was in new territory. For the first time in 4 attempts at the Arc of Attrition, my right knee was still working properly. I felt tired, worn out but positive. My mindset was 100% committed to finishing - I saw no reason at all that I couldn't do it.

Land's End (Checkpoint 3) – 55.2 miles

2018	**DNF**
2019	**01:32 - 02:10**
2020	**03:20 (DNF)**
2022	**02:24 – 03:14** *Target: 04:11 (1 hour 47 minutes ahead)*

Competitors Remaining: **191**

First 3 and last 3 people who completed the race:

	Race Time	Time of Day
Mark Darbyshire	09:35:32	Fri 21:35:42
Tristan Stephenson	09:40:43	Fri 21:40:53
Dave Phillips	10:31:29	Fri 22:31:39
Tarne Westcott	16:37:26	Sat 04:37:36
Iain Walker	16:50:29	Sat 04:50:39
Dylan Gould	16:55:07	Sat 04:55:17

I went through the doors of the Land's End Hotel at 2:24am. I was almost an hour behind my 2019 time, but my knee was working - I'd take the slower time and be able to carry on any day of the week!

Land's End is an important checkpoint. It's over half the distance of the race, and you have access to your drop bag. It's the middle of the night, so you're very ready for a stop. Without some prior planning, it's easy to waste a lot of time here. And it turns out, even with prior planning it's easy to waste a lot of time here.

The Arc crew are superbly organised. On the approach to the hotel, the valet went on ahead so as Pip & I went through the door, our drop bags were ready and handed straight to us. By the time I sat down in a seat I had a cup of tea and a bowl of chilli, rice and cheese on the way. I opted for tea at this point as a break from the coffee - I'd bolster my caffeine intake with a coffee just before leaving, but for now a sugary tea was spot on (I only ever have sugar in drinks during races, I normally find it disgusting but after hours of running a sugary cup of tea tastes fantastic!).

After 30 seconds of fumbling around with the drawstring on my drop bag I was in, grabbing the first plastic bag at the top. It didn't hold much - a USB charger and the cable for my watch - and that was the first thing I did. My watch battery had dropped from fully charged to 67%, which was suggesting a very decent battery life. But I'd only been using the mapping on the watch for about half the time - since Porthleven - and I'd also been trying to switch away from the map screen as often as possible to conserve the battery (continually drawing the map on the screen as you run takes a big chunk of the battery). Although it wasn't critical that I charged the watch, I wanted to make sure I had the flexibility to be able to use the map for the rest of the race without concern for the battery, and sticking it on charge was quick and easy.

Next out was my nutrition bag. The plan had been for a complete swap at this point. My "on-the-run" food in the front pocket should have been exhausted between Penzance and Land's End, and my top-up supply in the back was due to last from the start to Land's End. Basically, I shouldn't have any food left in my pack as I should have eaten it all. That was not the case. I took out bars, nuts, sticks, sachets and more bars from both bags. I had been absolutely rubbish at eating, consuming no more than a quarter of what I'd intended, and really *needed* to be better. I fiddled through the bags a bit, dumping a lot of sweet food and swapping it out for savoury - nuts, Pepperami sticks etc, and loaded up my race vest.

Next, my head torch batteries. Like the watch, this was probably unnecessary, but I'd rather take 60 seconds in the warmth of an aid station to change batteries than 5 minutes of mucking about in the dark, wind and rain of the coast path. At this point, I noticed my rear red flashing light had stopped flashing. I turned it on again, and it flickered a few times then died again. Luckily, I had a spare in my race vest, so I did a quick swap and set it going again now so as not to forget.

My tea and chilli had arrived, and all my gear was spreading around in quite a big area in front of me, under my chair and encroaching on the space of the people next to me. Mind you, we were all the same, everyone understands, and we all just quietly get on with our mid-race maintenance routines.

The chilli was delicious! As was the tea, and it was nice just to stop faffing for a minute and get some food in. Although I did end up pouring some odd Mountain Fuel Ginger powder into my water bottle and asking for them to be filled while eating - you can't waste time doing just one thing at a time!

Next was the big decision. In my drop bag I had a complete change of clothes, including socks. Could I be bothered? Swapping socks was a massive pain in the arse, but I thought it might just give me a boost, the feeling of fresh feet even for a few minutes is one of those tiny but important luxuries in an event like this. OK then, let's get this done.

Unclip gaiters, which in itself was a pain as they're not designed for my shoes so they are very tight to release. Then shoes off, conscious of the mud going everywhere. The Peregrine STs have a quick-release lace system, so at least undoing and redoing the shoes is quick and easy. Outer Drymax socks off. Now the worrying bit - the soaking wet inner Injinji toe socks off. How much of my foot would come off with them? Would a toenail or two pop off? Would I still have 10 toes attached?

They came off, and my feet stayed mostly together. I deliberately didn't take a good look at my toes and soles. They were all painful and I didn't want to know what state they were in; I find it better to be ignorant of these things when running along. I did slap some more Trench cream on my feet though, and then began the task of trying to get the Injinji toe socks onto wet, swollen feet. It's not easy at the best of times but trying to guide my toes into the individual little pockets was pretty damn uncomfortable. I gave up with the little outer toes - they were so swollen and blistered that they just refused to get in the holes. I really hoped that was an OK decision... it's not something you know if you can get away with until a few hours later, and there wasn't a lot more I could do about it.

Once those inner socks were on, the rest was easy and before long I was back to being properly shod and gaitered but with fresh clean socks. It felt... exactly the same as it had before I started. I didn't get any lovely warm feeling of my feet being cuddled by new socks. It just felt like I'd wasted 10 minutes. Oh well, it was done now, and a few minutes of my feet not being in wet socks was almost certainly a good idea.

An easier decision was to swap my top – that bit was simple. Off with the t-shirt, off with the base layer, on with the fresh new base layer which really *did* feel much nicer, and then a different t-shirt on top. I pondered whether to put my coat on at this point but decided against it. I knew it would be cold when I stepped out the door, but I figured that within a mile or so I'd have warmed up again, so the plan was just to head out in my base layer and t-shirt and play it by ear.

As I was changing, I heard a voice with a distinctive Liverpool accent next to me that I recognised. I turned, and asked "did you DNF here in 2020?"

"Yes mate! I remember you," he said. Two years before, we'd both slowly walked the section from Minack to Land's End over a good number of hours, both with very similar knee conditions stopping us running, and at Land's End stopping us racing completely. I'm 99% sure his name was Peter Brislen[16].

I think I was done. I asked for a cup of coffee to drink before I left and started packing everything back into the drop bag. I unplugged my watch - it was up to 85% which I figured should let me use the maps all the way to the end without concern. Actually, if I'm honest, I didn't really do any calculations on how long it would last - it was what it was and I partly hoped it would last, and partly thought I'd just stick it on charge again if needed, dangling it off my pack with the charge cable attached. My coffee arrived, and I took the opportunity to pop a couple more paracetamol. I was keeping an eye on time between the pills as I know you're not supposed to have them more often than every 4 hours, and not more than 8 in a 24 period. It was about 5 hours since I last had any paracetamol, and the next were due sometime around midday when I got to St Ives.

I handed my drop bag back to the Arc crew and went off to find Pip. He was at the far side of the room, packing his last few bits away. He looked quite unwell. I mentioned the paracetamol I'd just had, and he thought that was a good idea so got some out of his pack and had a couple… which immediately disagreed with him and he rapidly headed off in the direction of the toilet.

While I was waiting, I perused the array of snacks on offer at the food table. I ate a couple of bits of watermelon and grabbed

---

[16] For the rest of this story, I'm calling him Peter, so apologies if it's not right!

a wrapped brioche roll. I was about to pick up a pack of generic salt and vinegar crisps when I spied *Fish & Chips*! I hadn't had those since I was a kid - little fish-and-chip shaped things, a sort of hybrid between a crisp and a biscuit, with a strong salt and vinegar flavour. In my bag they went, I'd look forward to those!

Pip came out the toilet with a spring in his step, and although he looked a bit pale, he was smiling and said that he felt a lot better now. When your stomach goes haywire in an event like this, a jolly good "rainbow smile" can be just the thing to sort you right out!

At 3:14am we said our thanks and goodbyes to the fantastic Angels and headed out, a sign of what was to come hinted at by the lady firmly holding the door open for us against the wind.

I felt like I'd been fairly efficient in the checkpoint - I'm not sure I could have done things much faster without feeling like I was rushing. But overall, it had taken 50 minutes from entering to leaving, which was a lot longer than I had planned. Having said that, with the lack of timings on my watch, I didn't really have any schedule to keep other than to make sure I was ahead of the cutoffs. I had to be at Pendeen - about 10 or 11 miles away - by 8am, and I was sure I could make that without any issue.

CHAPTER 9
Land's End to Pendeen

It was cold. The wind was gusting in from the sea, and when it blew it sent a chill right through me despite the general warmth of the air, which was still around 11°C. I had contemplated whether to put my jacket on in the aid station, but decided against it, thinking I would warm up quite quickly, but I was beginning to wonder if I'd made the right decision. My hands were freezing so I started the process of putting gloves on. The Leki poles are brilliant, with their glove/clip system, but it does make it a bit of a nuisance if you want to put warm gloves on or take them off. I un-velcro'd the Shark gloves and found that instead of taking them off, I could slide them up my wrist while putting my Rab gloves on, then slip the pole-gloves back down again and velcro them back in place. To add to the warmth, I took my buff from its storage spot on my right wrist and put it around my neck, as well as digging out and putting on my warm hat which involved taking off my head torch for a moment.

All in all, it was a bit of a pain to get warmer. And what made it more annoying was that within 5 minutes - as predicted - I was too hot. The wind was blowing, but it wasn't as cold as I initially thought having just stepped out of the warmth of the checkpoint. And what's more, the undulating terrain meant that you were only in the full force of the wind occasionally, the rest of the time it was back to being nice and warm. Off came the hat, off came the gloves, and minutes later the buff went back on to my wrist.

Sennen – 56.7 miles

Year	Time	
2018	DNF	
2019	02:32	
2020	DNF	
2022	03:32	*Target: 05:10 (1 hour 38 minutes ahead)*

Competitors Remaining: **178**

Still, all that buggering about with hats and gloves had passed the time between Land's End and Sennen and before I knew it, I'd passed the First & Last House[17], headed down the steps into the town and was on the road towards the car park at the northern end. As you enter the car park, the coast path heads up a gentle slope on the right-hand side. It's easy to miss, and when I'd got here before there was a marshal guiding us the right way. So, I was slightly confused when we got to what looked like a

---

[17] The house, on Dr Syntax's Head is actually the furthest point west that the coast path goes. If you sneak further out onto Peal Point, you'll be as far west as you can go in England or Wales, but you'd have to head to Corrachadh Mòr in the Scottish Highlands to get to the most western point in the UK.

toilet block at the far end of the car park. Realising what had happened, I was about to turn back when Pip pointed out that there was a small set of steps up to the path, so we headed up and thankfully were straight back on the route round Whitesand Bay and on towards Gwynver beach.

Pip was feeling a lot better after sorting his stomach out, and he was picking up speed that I didn't really feel like I had at this moment. I wasn't feeling very chatty either, so slowed a little as he went off into the distance. Sometimes it's nice just to be alone, and I do have a particular love of the Land's End to Pendeen section... although I think that's mostly retrospective as I do remember loving it a little less while actually being out there on that night.

At Land's End, I'd swapped my music from the heavier Bring Me the Horizon to the more melodic *The Seldom Seen Kid* by Elbow. With darkness all around, waves crashing to the left and huge granite mounds to the right, Guy Garvey was doing his best to make me appreciate how lucky I was to be where I was right now:

> *Well, anyway, it's looking like a beautiful day*
> *So, throw those curtains wide*
> *One Day Like This a year would see me right...*

There was a lot more sand in this section than I remembered, to the point where at Gwynver Beach I wondered if I was going the right way. I checked my watch, and it wasn't clear as to whether I should be on the beach or further inland to the right, but I couldn't see a clear alternative to where Pip and a few other people were ahead on the sand, so I sucked it up and carried on. After some trudging on the soft sand, I saw the section that I was expecting and headed up to the right towards the dunes at the back of the beach and on to firmer ground.

Carrying along the path through fields of rocky boulders past Aire Point, I kept looking out for the huge granite outcrop that you have to climb over which I remembered was coming up. I assumed it would have some grand sounding Cornish name, but I didn't know what it was, so I named it Gerald as I was running along - I've since found that it's called *Carn Creagle*, which I like even more than Gerald. The rocks on the path meant most of the time I was concentrating on the ground, but I kept looking up and, in the distance, seeing oppressive granite structures rising out the gloom. But each one turned out to be off to the right of the path and I passed by with no climbing needed.

Then up ahead I spotted Gerald/Carn Creagle - the path running up to and over the middle of the big outcrop. Despite knowing the path, and what was coming, I managed to mistakenly head too low and round the left side of the carn. As I reached the first part of the climb up, I saw Pip on the rock above me. He called down asking whether this was the right way. Nope, but the right way would have involved going back round to the other side and this looked... well, it looked a bit sketchy to be honest. But it was sometime after 4am and I didn't fancy tracing my way back even a few metres. And Pip was pretty much at the top, so I unclipped my poles and started climbing up. The rock was steep, with no points to hold but it was dry and I just had to hope that my shoes would grip otherwise I was going back down, probably considerably further down than where I started from. As I got to the top of the first rock, Pip was climbing over the last and onto the path. I followed up, and once there it was clear the route we should have taken. But it was done now, and off we went again, Pip heading off at a faster pace into the distance again.

As I mentioned before, I had very fond memories of this section from previous runs, but this time I was starting to sink into a bit of a low. For the first time in any ultra, I was missing company. I usually like to run on my own, especially at night. I'm happy with my own company, and sometimes it's a bit too much effort to try and hold a conversation or a little uncomfortable to run at someone else's pace - either a little too fast or a little too slow. But right now, I was feeling a bit sorry for myself.

When you start feeling low, little things begin to annoy you. The spare water bottle in the back of my vest was starting to piss me right off. It was jammed into the stretch pocket on the back of the vest next to my coat, but the rubber top of the soft flask was poking out sideways and every time my arm went back it snagged a little. Nothing much, and it had probably been going on for hours, but those low times make things like this more apparent. I spent the next 5 minutes getting angrier as I kept trying to adjust the bottle so it wouldn't snag, then decided if I wasn't going to stop and take my vest off (which there was no way I was doing) then I'd just have to live with it.

In an attempt to try and change my mood up a bit, I thought about things that would cheer me up. I remembered my wife telling me that if I was getting down, if things were going wrong, I was to do a little "positivity dance". She was mostly taking the piss, and demonstrated a little skipping-while-running dance accompanied with exaggerated "jazz hands" while singing "Positivit-eeee!" But what the hell - I had nothing to lose and no-one else was around, so I skipped along, waving my hands around, singing away and breaking out into laughter. It certainly helped for a few minutes!

The path here was more inland, or at least felt more inland. The sea was still ever-present to the left and the sound of the waves on the rocks was continuous in the distance, but the path was winding up and down grassy hills that didn't feel immediately coastal. There were lots of lumps of granite and various bushes around, and the combination of darkness, head torch light and tiredness started triggering a familiar experience - hallucinations. Now, I'm not talking about totally tripping-out with rainbow skies and unicorns everywhere. These hallucinations are far more subtle, but much more than just normal imagination. Like a rock looking like a person lying on the ground - I mean *really* looking like a person on the ground - until you're almost on top of it when you see it's obviously a rock. They're not frightening, and I had quite a lot of fun with them later in the race, but they do show the sort of odd state the mind can get into when you're sleep deprived and have been running for hours.

I was obviously moving reasonably well still as I started closing in on a couple of people ahead. As I got to them, I said hello but then realised (as you do) that I desperately needed a pee, so I dropped back, switched off my head torch and tried not to soak my shoes. I took the opportunity to look up and see if I could see any stars as my light was off. I don't remember being amazed, so I can only assume there weren't many.

Light back on, I got moving again, turned left down a zig-zag section and then 2 minutes later entered the top of the Cot Valley. The route had changed from previous years a little further into the valley, and to make the new route clear MudCrew had put out some glow sticks, the first of which I saw directly ahead of me at the top of the valley side. Under normal circumstances, a glow stick would make you think that there might be something a little unobvious here and to take a look around. But at 4:41am, that didn't occur to me, and I just happily trotted down the most obvious path to the right. 2 minutes later, looking at my watch, it dawned on me that (a) I hadn't seen any more glow sticks, and (b) I was going the wrong way. I went back up (it's always up!) to the glow stick and peered over the valley edge to the right. And there they were, the very obvious line of glow sticks snaking down the steep side.

As I carefully descended the path towards the valley bottom, I couldn't help but notice the head torches of other runners further ahead. The path they were on was impossible to make out in the dark, but they seemed to be climbing up into the sky, as high as a mountain… I couldn't understand how they could be so high up, it looked ridiculous!

At the bottom is the Porth Nanven car park. In September 2017, a man fell down a hidden shaft, getting trapped 15 metres below ground and injuring his hip. Two hours later, the fire & rescue service, search and rescue team and ambulances were on the scene, working to rescue him, and some 5 hours after falling, the man was on his was to hospital. He was very lucky, and it shows how easy it is to have an accident in this area, with hundreds, maybe thousands of uncapped mineshafts dotting the countryside.

From the car park, the route took the road heading inland, a gentle incline back up the bottom of the valley. Glow sticks and big yellow arrows marked the route at this point, so no thought was required for navigation. Locomotion was simple too - it was too steep to run up (at least with the state of my legs at the time), but the surface was a flat, even road and not so steep as to not be able to make decent progress, so I settled into a fast walk up the hill. A sharp left - again clearly marked took me back almost 180 degrees continuing the climb, now on a rocky trail back towards the coast. By the top of the hill, I'd climbed around 200ft all on quite gentle slopes, and my headtorch was now one of those up in the sky above the valley as seen by anyone below.

Seemingly moments later, I saw a couple of cars parked on the side of the road in a layby. I remembered the location as the top of the hill leading down to Cape Cornwall, but I'd assumed I had another mile or two to go before there. Expectation vs reality again - I suddenly found I was a mile ahead of where I thought I was, and now I felt great again! I started the descent to Cape Cornwall.

It's not long - maybe ⅓ mile at most. But it's a descent that wiped the smile from my face. It wasn't too bad to start, rocks on the ground and a gradual slope which I was gently running down. I was wincing a little as the battered soles of my feet complained when I couldn't avoid the rocks. 2 minutes later, I was swearing profusely. Why couldn't Cornish people build a proper fucking road?! How difficult was it just to put some bloody tarmac down on the ground instead of these stupid rocks! I burst out laughing at the stupidity of my outburst, I *love* the coast path, I love the adversity, I love the difficulty, I love the natural-ness of the terrain and here I was wanting to bring everything I hate to it just to make it easier!

Finally, near the bottom, the rocks stopped and the road became... well, a road. As I rounded the sharp left bend, I exchanged jovial hellos with a couple of guys that I kept swapping places with along this section, one of whom was peeing into the bushes as you do! I went down (or was it up? I can't quite remember) some steps, round to the right and I was in Cape Cornwall car park. It was just after 5am.

Cape Cornwall – 61.7 miles

2018	DNF	
2019	04:06	
2020	DNF	
2022	05:04	*Target: 06:56* *(1 hour 52 minutes ahead)*

Competitors Remaining: 175

People love to quote the fact that Cape Cornwall is the only cape in England, but up until writing this I didn't actually know what a "cape" is. It turns out it's a headland where two bodies of water meet, so in the case of Cape Cornwall it's where the Atlantic splits either north up to the Bristol Channel and Irish Sea, or south to the English Channel. So now you know!

On the headland is a prominent chimney visible for miles around, part of the Cape Cornwall mine which extracted tin and copper from beneath the sea between 1836 and 1879. The official South West Coast Path goes up the headland and past this chimney, but the Arc route skips that small section.

The descent down to Cape Cornwall had been a problem. Firstly, it had caused me to lose my famed calm and start swearing (for clarity: the level of sarcasm here is off the scale), but more importantly, my right knee - the one that had been an issue in past Arc's - had started niggling. Just a little. It didn't hurt. I almost wouldn't have noticed it. But the tiny discomfort was there, and it was in the right (or wrong) place, just inside and below the knee. And it niggled just a bit more as I bent my leg. This was not good.

But also, it wasn't *bad*. It really wasn't hurting, it wasn't causing any issue at all, and there was every chance it would go away, right? In that car park, as I filled up water bottles and snuck in a cheeky cupful of coke, I contemplated what it might mean. My leg might stop working and fall off. Unlikely. It might hurt a bit. More likely. It might recover, or I might just be imagining it - again, unlikely, but possible. The common element between all these options - and every other option that may present itself - was that I could do precisely fuck all about it. So, what was the point in worrying? And there endeth the conversation, for now at least. I thanked the Arc Angels for being out at stupid o'clock to fill up my water bottles, and headed off up the hill, my poles clacking away on the ground.

The Kenidjack valley is very beautiful in the daytime, but a bit annoying at night. Over the mile or so after Cape Cornwall, you spend a chunk of time climbing, then drop back down to the valley floor and climb all the way back up again. I wasn't going quickly here, using my poles as much as possible trying to make sure my knee would last through the tough Pendeen-St Ives section that I knew was coming, but I was making steady progress.

At the top of the hill, the route flattened out and I saw some head torches a little way ahead looking like they were contemplating the route. After a brief discussion, they turned and headed up a small incline, a route marked between two ropes, which I think was right next to Kenidjack Cliff Castle, an iron age fort at the very top of the northern side of the valley. I caught up with them, and again said hi to Pip! It turned out he'd made a little more than a minor mistake going through the valley and ended up adding another large and unnecessary climb. But he was on the right route now, and on good terrain we all ran together as a group on a gravel track, heading to Botallack mines.

The sweeping light of Pendeen Watch lighthouse shone out to sea in the distance. Built in 1900, it aided ships in what was said to be one of the most dangerous stretches of coast in Britain. I was glad I'd be staying on land!

As we headed on the gravel path through the mining area, buildings shone in head torches left and right. The engine house of Wheal Edward, then the house and chimney of Wheal Owles passed, before heading into Botallack mines with chimneys and engine houses of one of the last working mines in Cornwall. On the base of the cliffs below and to the left - but totally invisible in the night - stood the Crown engine houses, right up there among my most favourite places in the world.

The path was mostly flat and easy going, and we headed past more ruins caught in the light of our head torches, heading through a little more built-up area at the National Trust Levant Mine and Beam Engine site and finally through Geevor Tin Mine which is the kind-of hub of the Cornish Mining World Heritage Site. Beneath the ground is almost 90 miles of tunnels, some stretching half a mile out to sea, and hundreds of metres below the ground.

As we left the mine area and headed into more shrubland, the group spread out and I drifted back. The final valley before Pendeen - which was a lot smaller than I remembered - came and went, and soon I was up on the road. Again, after far less road than I remember, the lights of cars and vans shone out in front at the car park in Pendeen. The time was 6:17am, and I'd never been further than here in all my attempts at the Arc of Attrition.

Pendeen – 65.6 miles

2018	**DNF**	
2019	**05:39**	
2020	**DNF**	
2022	**06:17**	*Target: 08:12* *(1 hour 55 minutes ahead)*

Competitors Remaining: **161**

First 3 and last 3 people who completed the race:

	Race Time	Time of Day
Mark Darbyshire	11:48:42	Fri 23:48:52
Tristan Stephenson	11:50:22	Fri 23:50:32
Dave Phillips	13:17:59	Sat 01:18:09
Armando Vieira	20:17:49	Sat 08:17:59
Dylan Gould	20:34:21	Sat 08:34:31
Iain Walker	20:48:49	Sat 08:48:59

CHAPTER 10
Pendeen to St Ives

So, I stopped. Gave up. DNF'd. The end.

Obviously not. Not this time. Why would I? My head wasn't singing and dancing, I wasn't having the "best time ever". My legs hurt. My problematic knee was on its way out again. My head was tired. I was knackered. But there was no thought of stopping. Not even remotely.

I was almost 3 hours ahead of the cutoff. I had a little under 8 hours to do the 13 miles to St Ives, and I figured I could crawl it in 6 hours. I knew roughly what was coming, and hence had a little apprehension. But… I was *excited* too! This was what it was all about! This was new for me, this was hard, this was the crux of the race… and this was me getting my bloody money's worth!

I found the Flying Angles van in the car park, did the standard water top up, cup of coke stuff, and got straight on with the rest of the Arc of Attrition.

Out of Pendeen, the first thing you come to is two big white rocks with "Private Property" painted onto them, and a road heading to the left down a hill. The GPS track on my watch showed that I should be going straight ahead between the rocks, but I was a little put off by the warning until I spied a couple of head torches coming back up the hill from Pendeen Watch Lighthouse, having gone the wrong way. So off into the Private Property I went, along with another guy who had caught up while I was dallying about navigation.

He was from Jersey, and the first thing he said was that he'd "just lost his wing man." His mate had bowed out at Pendeen, absolutely knackered. He did tell me his name, but my memory was starting to fall apart at this point so I can't remember it (I've even dug around in the names on the tracking website but nothing is ringing a bell). What I do remember is that he had a little bit of a knee problem and had borrowed poles. He'd never used them before but was really enjoying it and finding them useful. We chatted about runs we'd done, and he mentioned the 48 mile Round the Rock ultra in Jersey - basically the whole way round the island on terrain quite like the Arc course. I thought I'd heard of it, but turns out I was thinking of the Guernsey equivalent (GU36). He said it was quite similar, only the Jersey one was better. He went on to explain that everything in Jersey is better than Guernsey. So that was something new I learnt on the Arc 2022!

The early terrain on the feared Pendeen to St Ives section was actually not too bad. Normal trail, fairly flat, a bit of a switchback

150

and up a hill, a little bit of wet ground but still mostly flat. Further along, and down the hill to the back of Portheras Cove, across a wooden bridge over a stream I remembered filling water bottles from last time I was here, and back up a hill. Not flat or particularly easy, but nothing to fear here so far.

My knee was starting to make itself more known. By now, I knew it was definitely the same issue I'd had in the past, and I was a bit annoyed. Not because it would stop me - I'd get to St Ives, and then it should be easier from there - but because it was going to make the rest of the race less enjoyable than it could have been. I'm not saying a sore knee was the only reason I wouldn't be enjoying it, but it's a bit like a toothache - you can do other stuff, but it drops the enjoyment level down a notch. Having said that, the blisters on the balls of my feet that seemed to have appeared in the last 10 miles - caused by wet feet for the best of 50 miles so far - were already making things a bit less fun, so I figured this was just what I had to deal with now.

There's a general consensus that you should deal with things like blisters as soon as you notice them, otherwise they can become a big enough issue later to stop your race. Better to spend a few minutes now, than DNF later on. Well... fuck that. It was dark, it was wet, and it was windy, and there was nothing on earth that was going to get me to stop, take my pack off, dig around for my first aid kit, *take my shoes and socks off* and start on a bit of foot care!

I've had blisters before, to the point where in one race a blister was so painful that I figured it would be easier if it just popped, so I spent a good 30 seconds stamping with full force on my toe in an attempt to sort the bloody (literally) thing out! But so far - luckily - not once has a blister stopped my race. I've seen ones on other people that probably would have - especially where half their heel seems to have come off - but so far, I've managed to just have painful but tolerable blisters on my toes or, like today, on the balls of my feet.

I had this idea that if I knew that this section from Pendeen to St Ives would take 5-6 hours to do the 13 or so miles, it would be fine. I'd just do it. Time would tick by; the miles would pass and I'd get to St Ives before I knew it. But it doesn't work quite like that.

The first section was easier going - muddy paths, not too steep, through some fields, that sort of thing. Then with no significant feeling of change, the going gets tougher. The drops and climbs get bigger and more frequent. The rocks on the path mean every step isn't quite as easy as it should be. The progress is slow as you're switching back and forth, down valleys, over bridges, up steps. And that's where I was.

My tiredness was peaking as well – I'd been awake for over 24 hours and racing for over 18 of them. The hallucinations were more frequent, and I found that I could control them now. If I wanted to see an elephant, I'd just find a bush in the distance, caught in my head torch beam and think about it… and there was an elephant. Shapes morphed and changed, I saw bears, giraffes, badgers, dogs, chimneys (some of those might have been real), even a dolphin in the middle of the path at one point! There was a lot of talk on Facebook post-race about lots of mice in this area - it was either a mass hallucination or there really *were* loads of mice - but that was one thing I didn't see any of.

If I squinted and really imagined it, the horizon became faintly visible around 6:40am - definitely nautical twilight rather than civil twilight[18]. Ten minutes later, out of the corner of my eye I kept catching white glimpses but every time I turned to look there was nothing. A few minutes later it was clear that I was seeing the foam of the waves crashing into the rocks, but only peripherally. By 7am I could clearly make out hills and rocks in the distance.

Daybreak had been something I was looking forward to. There's always talk of a second wind, a lightness of step and burst of motivation when the sun comes up, and I was beginning to desperately need it.

I know that you're not supposed to do this, but calculations were whirring around in my head. If I could leave St Ives by 12pm, then at 15-minute mile pace I could walk the last 23 miles and be in with a gold buckle in under 30 hours. My watch ETA had been showing 10:27am at St Ives early on but was dropping

---

[18] Nerd fact alert: Sunset/sunrise is the point where the centre of the sun's disc hits the horizon. Civil twilight is 6 degrees below (about the time streetlights should turn on), nautical twilight is 12 degrees below (and the point where you should just about be able to see a ship on the horizon), and astronomical twilight is 18 degrees below.

away to almost 11am now. And as the excitement faded and realism crept in, I realised that 15 minutes miles in the last section – for almost 6 hours non-stop - was totally unrealistic. I was exhausted and beginning to fall apart, and I'd barely covered 3 miles of the Pendeen to St Ives section, a fair chunk of which had been easy.

The terrain lightened, and I toyed with the idea of turning off my head torch. The trail was solid but windy (actually, windy as well – as in it *wound* around a lot of corners, and the *wind* was blowing!), always going up or down, always twisty, rocky and irritating. There was no flow, no rhythm, just a staccato plod. Soon, it was clear I didn't need the head torch and I switched it off, but rather than the joy of daylight it just cast me into a grey gloom on a terrain that seemed to amplify the greyness.

At half past seven, some 3 miles on from Pendeen, I passed Bosigran. Around here, flints from the late Stone Age have been found, and there's the remains of cairns and a cliff castle from the Bronze Age. Another mile further on, above Porthmeor Cove, the path dropped to the stream in the valley and then rose to Porthmeor Point. I was now on the continuous rollercoaster of this north Cornwall coast path.

My knee would have been fine if the terrain was flat and easy, but this was the polar opposite of flat, easy terrain. Occasional twists brought progressively worsening winces of pain, but in between it was fine. There was still no reason to stop, I just hoped that I could get to St Ives and still be mobile - if so, I was confident that I could finish as it was flat from St Ives. I mean, I hadn't actually checked that it was flat, but it must be, right?

Time runs differently between Pendeen and St Ives. After what felt like 20 minutes of walking, I'd look at my watch and the distance covered would be a quarter of a mile. It just felt so slow... and I kept starting to think of the 23 miles to do from St Ives but knew that was a bad route to go down, so quickly changed the subject in my head every time that thought came up.

I passed fields to the right as the path headed back out towards the sea on the top of Treen Cliff, then passed Gurnard's Head on the left. I had been looking out for this headland as I knew it was a good chunk of the way between Pendeen and Zennor and I was waiting to tick it off mentally, but I actually had no idea I'd passed it until reaching Zennor sometime later.

The single remaining wall of the ruin of the mediaeval Chapel Jane came and went, it's "Danger of Death" sign bright yellow against the green, brown and grey of the background. Round Boswednack cliff, behind Porthglaze cove and heading out around Carnelloe Long Rock, I continued on the heavily undulating, wet and rough path.

I was getting overtaken by people regularly here. It wasn't an issue because I didn't care about my position in the race, but it made me feel slow, like I was dropping back and going below average pace. The ETA on my watch for St Ives was well past 11am now, and I wasn't even at Zennor yet. The wind was strong, sometimes blocked by hills but sometimes in full force seemingly coming from all directions. At one point, a sudden gust of wind almost blew me off a stone bridge I was crossing and into the stream below.

All in all, I was having a really shit time mentally. The terrain was tough, but I knew this. It just also coincided with a massive emotional low, the breaking of a grey day, having been awake for over 25 hours and racing for more than 19 of them, not having eaten enough and it still be a long time - a good number of hours - before I'd get any respite at a checkpoint. I think, in hindsight, the lack of eating was becoming quite a big problem. My energy levels were low, my enthusiasm and motivation almost non-existent, and if I'd been snacking - a job made more difficult by hands being occupied with poles - my spirits may have been higher.

Along the top of Carnelloe cliff I went, then around 9am I crossed the stream down Trewey Cliff, over a bridge with a poignant story attached. A couple of weeks before the start of the Arc, Toby Lowe posted a photo of the bridge on Facebook, along with the following:

If you get to Zennor (on both the Arc and Arc50), you'll cross this bridge. If you'll allow me, there is a small story attached to it. Back in 2009, I was working as a ranger in Penwith. In the April of that year, the north Penwith coast was hit by one of the worst floods in living memory. It was absolutely appalling (and unfortunately resulted in two fatalities). Practically every bridge between St Ives and Gurnards Head was washed away and we had to shut this section of coast down for about 4 months.

The bridge at Zennor was one of the many that we replaced. It's also the largest bridge in West Cornwall. 15 metre bearers of French Oak (we couldn't source them from the UK) - the original bridge was 8 metres long but the flood waters had carved a massive new channel. Now, whilst I pranced around in a pick up pretending to be Ray Mears, the real hard graft was being done by the guy heading up our work gangs called Al Green (known by one and all as Big Al). Al was one of the finest Cornish men I have ever met. He loved this coast with all his heart and knew it like the back of his hand. He was also a close friend and someone that I not only respected, but also looked up to. Unfortunately he passed away last year. Many of the bridges that you will cross on your journey were built by Al, but this is his finest. It was also an absolute bugger to get the materials down to, but somehow Al worked out how to do it, he always did. So if you would be so kind (and if you remember) please raise a virtual glass as you cross the Zennor bridge and say a 'cheers Al'. He'll hear ya, I'm sure of it

I got the bridge wrong (I thought it was an earlier one), but I did raise a virtual glass to Al on the route. Had I got the right bridge, it might have knocked me out of feeling quite so sorry for myself, the thought of him doing some proper hard graft getting that bridge built.

After crossing the bridge, I trudged very, very slowly up some steps. Part way up was a bench and I half sat, half fell down onto it, the pack on my back crashing into the seat. I sat there, contemplating the situation. I knew I had to get going again quickly, but I just wanted a 2-minute break to clear my head. I figured I should take the opportunity to try and eat something, so I snapped off part of an SIS chocolate flapjack. A serious amount of chewing, some added water, and a mental struggle to not throw it up as I swallowed and I had a minor victory, at least that was some food in the system.

I got up from the bench and continued up the last of the steps, not realising that I'd actually reached Zennor. There were people, crew members for other runners clapping and congratulating. I was in something of a daze, I asked if this was Zennor and the lady I'd asked had to confirm with the guy next to her (so it wasn't just me that was confused!) but yes, I was there!

Zennor – 72.7 miles

2018	**DNF**	
2019	**DNF**	
2020	**DNF**	
2022	**09:12**	*Target: 12:12 (2 hours ahead)*

Competitors Remaining: **150**

First 3 and last 3 people who completed the race:

	Race Time	Time of Day
Mark Darbyshire	13:23:57	Sat 01:24:07
Tristan Stephenson	13:38:59	Sat 01:39:09
Dave Phillips	15:46:33	Sat 03:46:43
Russell Wakefield	23:19:22	Sat 11:19:32
Dylan Gould	23:22:10	Sat 11:22:20
Iain Walker	23:43:18	Sat 11:43:28

Alphabetically the last parish in Britain, Zennor is the big milestone in the Pendeen to St Ives section. It's over half way, and most people consider the Pendeen to Zennor section tougher than the second part to St Ives. So mentally I felt like I had broken the back of this. I had less to do than I'd already done.

There's a sign at Zennor, a mile-marker. I've looked it up and it says "Pendeen Watch 7 miles, St Ives 6 miles". Thankfully, I didn't see this as I thought I had about 4 or 5 miles to go, and I think just the sight of 6 miles would have broken me. I just tried not to think that it was still going to be something like 2½ hours to cover the next section.

Now, I mentioned above that the section between Zennor and St Ives is easier than the first part from Pendeen, but I didn't know that for a fact. I'd heard a few people mention it, and decided to not over-analyse but just go with it. The hope was that if I assumed it would be easier, then it would *feel* easier, as I'd be in a better place mentally. So off I went, a little lifted by the

159

support at Zennor, and a little happier entering what I now assumed was an easier section.

It didn't take long for that thought to be knocked out of me. There's a difference between "easier" and "easy". Maybe it was the former, but it certainly wasn't the latter. I was quickly going up and down the same winding, narrow, rocky, muddy paths and foot-soaking boggy sections.

From Zennor, the path goes around the back of Porthzennor Cove, where the terrain changes from hard fine-grained rocks to coarse-grained granite, and the path gets grittier. The huge blob of granite that makes up most of West Penwith[19] starts here but didn't quite make it as far as Zennor head.

In order to cope with the full length of a race like this, I was breaking it down into personally significant milestones. Along this section I had 3 key points in mind from the last time I passed here a few months before. Today, the first point I should reach would be a wooden fence on the side of the path where, back in September, I had met a lady of around 65 who was confidently walking along the path with a stick on her morning walk. Not the sort of typical terrain you'd expect someone with a wooden walking stick to be walking on, but she had it nailed and told me she did it every day! The second milestone was a set of boulders which I remembered having to climb over, a nice bit of

---

[19] West Penwith, also known as the Land's End Peninsula, is essentially the west of Cornwall from St Ives in the north and Penzance in the south. There's an inland chunk missing in the south, but it does include all the coastline.

clambering fun to break up the walking. And the third was a set of big stepping stones, somewhere pretty close to St Ives.

The Zennor Time Distortion Field was working well, and despite continuous forward motion my progress according to my watch was glacial. One or two toys were currently being thrown out of the pram, and I was descending into a pit of sorrow. Poor me... why was it so hard? What was the point? Stupid terrain, why couldn't it just be flat? And dry? But despite being tired, mentally and physically, I knew this wasn't going to achieve anything. Time to wind it in, cheer up, and focus. Remembering my mantra: "how you feel doesn't matter", it was time to put up and shut up, quit the pity party and get the job done.

I'm conscious of sounding quite negative all through this section. It's worth pointing out that while my brain was having a strop, the terrain around here - while tough - was stunning in a barren, desolate way. The coastline weaves in and out and up and down constantly, and there's regular views of beautiful beaches or rocky coves. The sea is almost glowing green-blue in areas, an amazing contrast to the rocks and vegetation. The scattered granite, derelict buildings and steep slopes just create a totally unique area.

But... it does all sort-of blend into one after a time. And when the terrain all looks the same, unless it's your local stomping ground it's very difficult to know where you are. Those key points - the fence, the boulders and the stepping stones - were really my only sense of progress. I have no recollection of seeing the fence, so that must have gone by either much earlier than expected in the dark, or while I was in a daze or having some kind of tantrum.

But the rocks to climb over, I couldn't miss those. A bit over a mile out from Zennor Head, the terrain became lumpier, bigger granite rocks around the path, and then I was faced with a much longer and more technical section of rocks to climb over than I remembered. My memory had compressed this section to one single rock to climb up, but in reality, it took 5 minutes or so to find a route through, clip and unclip poles (they're really not helpful when climbing rocks!), and lift tired legs with tired triceps up and around a dozen or so big boulders. It was sort-of fun though, a different feeling, something other than just plodding along. And it ticked off the 2nd of my 3 milestones on this section, feeling like I was making progress.

Over the previous hour or so, I'd been swapping places with Peter, the guy from Land's End. We both had our heads down in our own worlds, struggling away. It seemed on some sections I caught up with him, maybe due to navigation errors on his part, and later he'd catch up with me when I was struggling to move at any kind of pace.

Half an hour later and a mile further down the track, out to sea on my left were the rocky islands of The Carracks, named after the Cornish word for rock. The largest of the islands is known as Seal Island due to the grey seals that live there.

In July 1916, a huge bank of fog caused problems for shipping along the coast, and the 3,800-ton coal-laden steamship *Enrico Parodi* ran aground 300 metres away from the Carracks. Initially there was hope of re-floating the ship, but while being towed a minor leak split open and the ship sank, remaining there 28 metres below the surface, today being a diving attraction.

Twenty minutes later, I passed a trig point at Carn Naun. The idea to put trig points on the top of prominent hills and mountains began in 1935, part of a plan to improve the accuracy of maps which took the next 30 years. The brass plate on top of trig points is used to mount a theodolite which can measure the angles between trig points very accurately, allowing measurements of the whole country with an accuracy of around 20 metres.

The "Merry Harvesters" stone circle was visible beside the path another half a mile or so later – although what you actually see is most likely a Victorian reconstruction of the original ancient stone circle.

As I research all these points, I wish I'd known about them *before* the Arc. There are so many interesting points along this part of the route, and I could have had something every mile or so to tick off as I made my way to St Ives!

The path goes past Hor Point, taking me with it. During the Second World War, this was home to a radar station to monitor shipping and low-flying aircraft. The antenna had to be swung back and forth to detect reflected signals, and movement was originally powered by wheel-less bikes, ridden by members of the

Women's Auxiliary Airforce! After the war someone had the bright idea of blowing the place up with explosives, sending rubble down the hill, some of which sits on the coast path and in the undergrowth above.

Just before 81 miles into the Arc of Attrition, a bit after 11am, I reached my 3rd milestone - the stepping stones. I remember in past visits these being essential for walking along this section without disappearing into the mud, but today there was moisture on the ground around them, a bit of mud, but it really was very dry in comparison to previous visits. I skipped my way along these, again far more of them than I remembered, and by the end it was more of a lurch than a skip, but still, milestone 3 ticked off - I must be nearly at St Ives now!

I chatted briefly with a guy who seemed to be moving well and had caught me up. He knew the area well, and as we chatted a little about the conditions, he said he'd never seen it so good around here at this time of year. Places that were usually large areas of bogland were mostly dry, and there was minimal mud to get through. I dread to think what this section must be like on a bad year!

You can tell you're approaching civilisation by the number of "normal" people you start seeing - a family group of 4 went past, and I had a quick chat with them. The lady told me that the next 5 minutes to Hellesveor was "quite tough" then it got easier as you went on into St Ives. If she thought that was tough, she's going to have a very interesting day going West!

Down a grassy hill and the pace was picking up. There was excitement in the air, runners ahead and behind had a determination and positivity in their movements. This hellish section was almost done.

And then there was tarmac! That beautiful sight - flat easy terrain signalling no more effort required and I'd be in St Ives almost immediately. Funny how your brain gets it so wrong… The tarmac path went up, quite significantly up. And kept going up, for a lot more than "no distance at all" which is what I was expecting. At the top, the town was clearly visible, although a little further away than I would have liked (i.e., it wasn't right there, right in front of me, now!).

The tarmac footpath meets a road, and sat on the wall was Johnny, surrounded by his family. I'd been swapping places back and forth with him since yesterday afternoon. As a little group of us went past, he said that he was going to DNF at St Ives. I stopped and took a moment to suggest he should take a break at the checkpoint and then get out and keep going. Even if it feels completely shit now, get out the checkpoint and keep moving otherwise you'll regret it. I didn't say it, but in the past almost everyone who gets to St Ives by the cutoff also gets to the end, and we were over 2 hours ahead so there was loads of time in the bank. I checked up on how he did after the race, and I think he did make it out of St Ives but it looks like he finished at Hayle - good on him for getting going out the checkpoint, but he must have just had enough.

The road went around the back of Porthmeor beach and being 11:30am on a Saturday it was quite busy with people. Normal life goes on, which is easy to forget when you've spent the last 5 hours in the wilderness, and 12 hours before that on a path in the dark.

The road curved around to the right, then entered the classic narrow streets of the town. The track on my watch was useful here, and at the bottom of a hill as the road met the coast, I could see the path doubled back. There were a few confused looking runners who obviously didn't have the benefit of a GPS track and were looking baffled. I told them it doubled back, but I'm not sure they believed me until I rounded the corner and saw the Arc Valets ready and waiting. I shouted back and we all headed around. I wasn't running at this point due to my knee, but I could fast-walk the streets of St Ives chatting with the valet. Incidentally, Colin Bathe did a bit of Strava-stalking[20] after the event and found one particular valet at St Ives who'd covered 11 miles during the back-and-forth trip of guiding runners to the aid station, certainly not an easy day out!

Turning into the very Cornish sounding Street-An-Pol, the aid station at the Guildhall was a little way up on the right, and I stormed through the doors like I owned the place! It was 11:37am - it had taken just under 3 hours to go from Pendeen to

[20] Strava is a social media network for cyclists and runners, where you can upload your runs and get "kudos" and comments, join clubs, create routes and all sorts of other exciting stuff… if you like that sort of thing at least.

Zennor, then around 2 hours 20 minutes from there. It had felt like about 3 weeks.

	St Ives (Checkpoint 4) – 78.6 miles
2018	**DNF**
2019	**DNF**
2020	**DNF**
2022	**11:37 - 12:04** *Target: 13:30* *(1 hour 53 minutes ahead)*

Competitors Remaining: **147**

First 3 and last 3 people who completed the race:

	Race Time	Time of Day
Mark Darbyshire	14:46:43	Sat 02:46:53
Tristan Stephenson	15:16:45	Sat 03:16:55
Dave Phillips	17:41:15	Sat 05:41:25
Tarne Westcott	1d 01:41:00	Sat 13:41:10
Jason Mitchell	1d 01:46:00	Sat 13:46:10
Iain Walker	1d 01:53:57	Sat 13:54:07

My nutrition strategy had gone out the window. I'd had about 400ml of sugary, ginger Mountain Fuel, a single bite of an SIS flapjack, a packet of Fish & Chips crisps and half a brioche roll over the 23 miles and 8 hours since Land's End. I felt mentally and physically exhausted and my stomach was rumbling, more than ready for some proper food.

The aid station crew were brilliant as usual. Before I'd sat down, I had a beef stew and cup of coffee on order, and moments later they were both on the table as I sat and started contemplating what I needed to fiddle around with in my pack. I wolfed down the beef stew, and shortly afterwards I had a bowl of vegetarian chilli with rice and cheese on the table in front of me as well. I could barely swallow a sweet chunk of flapjack on the path but give me real food and I could eat for Britain!

My water bottles were laying on the table waiting for me to add some more magic sugary powder - the one way I could be sure of getting at least some calories in while moving. Over the next 10 minutes as I was eating, I think 6 different Arc Angels saw the bottles on the table and asked if I wanted them filled, such was the attentiveness of the crew. It was a busy aid station, and yet, again, I felt like everyone was there just for me.

Without going into too much detail, over the preceding hours, I'd had a bit of an urge for the toilet. I didn't right at this moment, but as I was in the aid station, I thought I'd "give it a go", the sort of thing I'd say to my kids when they were younger! I didn't manage to do anything productive, but I do think that the rearranging of my multiple layers of clothing from hips down wasn't a bright idea and led to some significant discomfort in the buttock regions later down the line... Note to self - maybe bring the Squirrels Nut Butter into the toilet next time!

Back at the table, I chucked another couple of paracetamol in with some coffee, swapped my music over to the live *Familiar to Millions* album by Oasis and got those water bottles topped up having finally dug out and added some SIS power. The last thing I did was to dump the contents of the spare 500ml soft flask I'd been carrying since the start - the one that kept catching my arm – squash it down and shove it into the back of my vest. That was 500g of water I didn't need to be carrying any more.

With my vest back on and poles in hand, I headed out the door at 12:04pm, just over 24 hours since leaving Coverack yesterday afternoon, and with just under 12 hours to get to the end.

CHAPTER 11
St Ives to Porthtowan

I left St Ives just as Peter was leaving, so we headed out together. After the rest, things were a bit stiff getting going but it wasn't long before they loosened up as we headed along the flat, smooth road, such a change from the previous section.

My knee was quite unhappy now, the previous section taking quite a toll, but as long as I didn't bend it much then it was still pretty much pain free. Walking on the flat and even a slight up or down incline was not a problem, even if I picked the pace up. But anything technical - climbs, steps, twists etc - and it would be painful. I was pretty sure it would be OK getting to the end, I couldn't see my knee suddenly blowing out or degrading to the point where I wouldn't be able to move. And the issue I had in 2019 - where the opposite side glute gave up from overuse - shouldn't happen now as I was using poles, although I wasn't sure the same could be said for my triceps which were certainly feeling the extra work of those poles.

Wow, though! Not only was I the furthest I'd ever been in the Arc, past the well-known and feared Pendeen-to-St Ives section, but I was also past the last checkpoint. The distance remaining on my watch wasn't to a pit-stop, a checkpoint, a half-way point... but the end. The finish. The Arc, completed!

I got a tad carried away with this line of thought, then reminded myself I still had a little under 22 miles to go (which was nice, as until the point where I left the St Ives checkpoint, I thought it was 23 miles – another one of those small but wonderful wins).

Peter and I were chatting as we went along, looking out towards Godrevy point and the lighthouse about 4 miles away as the crow flies. It didn't look far, so even knowing that we didn't take a direct route and it was about 11 miles of walking, I figured we'd soon be there. I really was in a deluded state of mind since leaving that checkpoint!

I'd been telling myself - and Peter - that it was pretty much flat for a good chunk from St Ives. And if, by a good chunk, I meant about half a mile then that was true. It was road, but it quickly morphed into a steep uphill section, crossing the train track by Carbis Bay station, then dropping down again. I remember a while back when there were building works going on here the coast path ran through the middle of the rather nice Carbis Bay hotel (incidentally, the site of the 2021 G7 summit) - sweaty, smelly runners and walkers passing by the bathers enjoying some peace and quiet at the edge of the pool. I'm sure they were absolutely delighted that there was a right-of-way that had to be kept open running right through their hotel!

My knee meant I couldn't run, but my walking pace was fairly decent still, and Peter was having a bit of trouble keeping up so we said standard ultra-goodbyes: "I'll see you soon when you pass me!".

The path rounded the headland at the eastern side of Carbis Bay and continued on grass and sand behind Porthkidney beach, still following the line of the train track. The thing about trains is that they don't like to go up and down hills, so while the path was next to the trains, the path was pretty much flat ... so I was sort-of right about what I said from St Ives.

Turning a corner, I bumped into David Streeter, a guy I knew from back home who was along to support friends in the race. He took some photos and walked along with me for a few minutes for a chat. It's always nice to see an unexpected familiar face, it lifted my mood and gave me a boost. After a mile or so at the far end of West Cornwall Golf Club, the path turned to the right, crossed the train track and started heading south towards Hayle.

The route passed a church and onto the road and this was obviously a crew meeting point as there were lots of cars and runners around. As I passed the cars, one guy was just leaving his crew and heading along the road at the same sort of pace as I was walking, so we got chatting.

I'm not sure of his name, but we were chatting about how it was all going, about various races we'd done and what was left to do. He seemed to know the area, and at least confirmed that it was mostly road and stayed flat through Hayle. We hit the main

B3301, crossing over the River Hayle, at which point I was having a bit of shell-shock from the traffic. At no point from the start had there been this much noise, the closest being the bit through Penzance, but at 9pm it was quite different from 1pm on a Saturday afternoon!

I was making the most of the flat terrain here, and although I couldn't run, I was trying to keep my walking pace high. But it wasn't like last night in Marazion and Penzance - 13- or 14- minutes miles were pie-in-the-sky territory - I was working hard, but covering a mile in about 16 minutes.

A little outside the centre of Hayle, at a large agricultural looking building on the left, the wife (I assume) of the chap I was walking with pulled into the layby in a van and he stopped to do things you do when you have a crew, saying for me to go on and he'd catch up. He did say that the path went to the left in a minute, so I kept my eyes open.

I needn't have worried. The bloody great yellow sign with a black arrow pointing to the left removed most of the ambiguity about the route here. I duly headed north, off the pavement and down a path, enjoying the fact that I was following the official South West Coast Path instead of the boring old road - it's nice to follow a route done properly.

Thirty seconds later, as I lowered myself down a bit of collapsed path, wincing as my knee complained, and then headed right onto a brick strewn, narrow, overgrown and uneven path, I may have uttered a few curse words. I carried on along the edge of Carnsew Pool, avoiding falling into the murky water, tripping over bricks, getting snagged in barbed wire fencing or brambles and generally really enjoying not walking on a nice smooth pavement instead. Does my sarcasm come across ok here?!

It wasn't far. And it wasn't really difficult. The arrow to the right spelt relief, although I knew that I couldn't complain at a bit of uneven but flat terrain like this knowing there was still a good number of miles to come that would make this section look absolutely delightful.

Hayle – 84.2 miles

2018	DNF	
2019	DNF	
2020	DNF	
2022	13:40	*Target: 15:46* *(2 hours 6 minutes ahead)*

Competitors Remaining: 136

Once back on the pavement, I headed into Hayle, fortuitously timing the traffic lights by the big Asda perfectly and just walking non-stop across the road like a boss, then passed by the side of the impressive Angarrack viaduct. Originally built of wood in 1852 to carry the new railway, the current stonework was added sometime later and the viaduct fully refurbished in 2014 to prevent the internal woodwork rotting away. The viaduct was at the end of a water inlet, and once round to the other side, the race route went back towards the coast. On the left, after half a mile or so, was Philps Bakery, which according to the South West Coast Path Facebook group had a reputation for the best pasties on the whole of the coast path. Before the race, I had seriously contemplated calling in here on the way past to grab a pasty, and with it being 1:45pm on a Saturday it would have been perfectly reasonable… but I didn't. I was single-mindedly focused on getting to the end of the race, and it seemed like too big a thing to deal with: figuring out queueing, choosing, paying. And any delay - no matter how small - was inconceivable. So, it's on the list for next time in St Ives.

Further up the road, I crossed a road bridge, passed Hayle outdoor swimming pool and headed up North Quay towards the beach. It wasn't the prettiest road in the world, being essentially a massive building site, although there was one lone, old chimney, covered in greenery on one side, that caught my attention. Originally the site of the Calcining Works which extracted arsenic from the spoils of the local Wheal Lucy tin mine, it was later used by the local glass works and then ICI until 1973. All buildings on the site were demolished soon after except for the chimney, which stands as a reminder of the history in the area.

The track on my watch guided me left into what looked like a part of the construction site, but a big sign saying "Access to Beach" suggested I was going the right way. I headed along the progressively sandier road towards the beach, not quite sure what to expect. I took a right turn and was met with a granite marker labelled "Hayle Towans", *towan* being Cornish for sand dune.

At this point I was a bit confused. I knew of the "Dunes of Doom" which were a couple of miles before Godrevy. But I was what I estimated to be about 2½ miles before where they should have started. I couldn't be that wrong, could I?

The Dunes of Doom were so named as back when the Arc started in 2015 it was a bit of a challenge to navigate through this particular set of dunes - officially named *Upton Towans*. In recent years, granite markers have been added to guide coast-path users through, although there's still a little bit of scope for going the wrong way.

I'd assumed that the "doom" was not only the navigation complexity, but the terrain too - soft sand, tougher going, sand in your shoes, all that sort of thing... but no. It turns out the name is just from the navigation bit... So, Hayle Towans, Mexico Towans, Gwithian Towans and Godrevy Towans - covering a good couple of miles around Upton Towans - are also soft, sandy and duney... just not as *doomy*.

To be fair, they weren't particularly difficult to move over - a mix of grass and sand - but it was definitely a change from the pavement I'd been on for the last 6 miles since the checkpoint at St Ives. And being in an oddly pragmatic mood, what was I going to do? Just get on with it, that's what.

The first part was a bit sandy, up over a small hill, then the ground became more hard-packed and easier to move on as I went around the coast, past some public toilets and round the edge of a caravan park. It then turned back to what you'd describe as "classic dunes", a mix of hilly sand and spiky green grasses.

It was just past 2pm, and I'd covered 88 miles. A thought kept cropping up in my head, more frequently as the time went on - where were the Arc 50 runners? That race had started at 8:30am, so had been going for 5-and-a-half hours now. I had never actually looked at the timings for the Arc 50, but I assumed the front runners might be coming through round about now. I wasn't sure what pace they would be going at, but at 9-minute miles, the front runners should be passing me around now.

I've obviously got a sixth sense, some extra sensory perception. Yeah, let's go with that. Because as I looked behind, I saw a couple of runners coming along. I was heading through a narrow section of sand between grass growing on both sides, and conscious of not wanting to be in the way I put in a bit of a burst to get to a spot where I could pull to one side. I pulled over and congratulated them both as they went past. One guy looked as fresh as anything. The other looked like he'd died a few miles before - I'm not sure if it was down to effort or concentration, but he just looked... there's no other words for it: absolutely fucked![21]

A friendly voice called over from my right side, and I spotted a couple with a dog. It took me a second, but I recognised Steve Davis, a runner friend from back home! He'd mentioned before

---

[21] I found out later that what I witnessed was the subject of some controversy. I won't comment any more here and leave you to do your own research if interested.

the race that he was in the area on holiday and had come over to the Towans to watch a bunch of knackered runners doing the latter stages of the race. Although, to Steve, I doubt it looked like a race - I was walking across some sand at a singularly unimpressive pace.

We chatted a bit about the race, what it had been like so far and what was to come. Seeing a friendly face really boosted my mood again and chatting with Steve was brilliant. He ran ahead a couple of times and took a few photos on his phone, and soon it was time to say goodbye (his wife was now a fair distance behind with the dog!)

If you're ever experiencing a bit of doom, then I can recommend a GPS track on your watch to guide you through. The granite marker stones help too. Just follow those… except for the one that points in the wrong direction. Eventually, you'll cease to be bothered by doom as the general terrain flattens and the route becomes obvious, and just have to tolerate a few more dunes.

After Upton Towans, I went through a car park and passed some more toilets. There was a big sandy clearing in front of me, a fence running down the middle, but after that it wasn't all that obvious where the route went. I started following the track shown on my watch, until looking ahead I saw that it would take me right through the middle of a… well, a massive puddle, more of a pond in fact. I didn't fancy getting wet feet, but 27 hours and 90 odd miles in I wasn't in the mood for impromptu navigation adjustments.

I stopped for a second and took stock. The path took me through some water - enough to make my shoes very soggy. To the right was a fence and a lot more water, and swimming wasn't part of the challenge today. To the left was a gravelly area that curved around and joined up with the track, probably adding about 50 metres. Oh. That was easy.

I walked the long way round, adding about 50 metres. I went through a now obvious gap in the hill in front, took a bridge over the Red River and headed up a small set of steps to Godrevy car park.

Godrevy!

Just a place. But an important place. I'd covered about half the distance from the final checkpoint in St Ives to the end... the Arc of Attrition was almost done!

I was feeling on a bit of a high, so when I went up the steps to the car park and saw Stephen Cousins, I waved my arms around in front and said that it was all going well! He had the look on his face of someone slightly concerned for their own safety, having no clue at all who this idiot was that was shouting something about finishing at him! I wasn't very clear about being the guy who was on his fourth attempt, that he'd interviewed this morning (along with a hundred other people I'm sure), but I didn't care. I was happy - I was nearly finished!

Nearly finished... will I never learn?!

Up at the Arc van, I ceremonially dumped the disgusting sugary SIS crap that I had in one of my water bottles - I wouldn't need that any more as I only had about 10 minutes left, right? I refilled the bottle with water, had some more coke in my cup to keep the caffeine levels somewhere above "dangerously high" - the level I needed to keep my eyes open at this point, and got going. It was 3:15pm and I had 11.9 miles left to go.

Godrevy – 89.6 miles

2018	**DNF**	
2019	**DNF**	
2020	**DNF**	
2022	**15:28**	*Target: 17:44* *(2 hours 16 minutes ahead)*

Competitors Remaining: **131**

Just off Godrevy Point lies Godrevy island, home of the lighthouse and a focus of a stunningly beautiful view. Like most of the north Cornish coast, this was a lethal area for shipping and while many vessels had been lost, in November 1853 the *SS Nile* sank with the loss of all aboard. This tragedy was enough to trigger Trinity House[22] to build a lighthouse which was completed in 1859.

Heading out of the car park, the path starts climbing up to Godrevy Point, Navax Point and onto the North Cliffs. I'd taken a quick look at the elevation profile on my watch to see what was coming up, and the hill took us up about 200ft and was then mildly undulating for a fair chunk of the remainder. A little alarm bell rang about the last few miles, but I decided to look away and ignore that bit.

As I climbed the hill, I ended up alongside another runner, Jim Preston, and we got chatting about the usual stuff. We were both absolutely knackered, but also determined to get to the end - that wasn't negotiable. But the pace… the pace felt glacial. Walking along, even at what felt like a fast pace (it wasn't really), we both figured that we had another 4 hours or so of this. When, on a normal day, you can cover 7 or 8 miles in an hour, it's a bit soul destroying to be doing less than half of that with such a desperate need to get to the end.

---

[22] Trinity House is the official authority for lighthouses in England, Wales, the Channel Islands and Gibraltar. It was formally known as (wait for it…) *"The Master, Wardens and Assistants of the Guild Fraternity or Brotherhood of the most glorious and undivided Trinity and of St Clement in the Parish of Deptford Strond in the County of Kent"*

The weather wasn't helping. The wind had died down a bit through the town but was picking up now we were on the top of the cliffs. It was starting to feel colder, the sky was grey, the air was damp and the even the scenery seemed a bit melancholy.

But the conversation helped, as it always does. Time passes quicker when you're chatting. And I try to be positive when chatting so as not to bring anyone down, and in turn I think that makes me feel more positive. Sometimes that self-talk inside your head can get a bit gloomy but if you try to put a positive spin on it and say it out loud, the thoughts get more cheerful.

I did wonder what the point of this bit was though. I mean, I knew I could walk the final 11 miles. So why bother actually doing it? The problem of the Arc was solved, the back of it broken, I could finish no problem. Why did I need to prove it?

But then... a DNF? This late? For no reason other than I'm feeling a bit tired and there's a bit more work to do? Nah, bollocks to that. It might be miserable, but I'm getting this shit done. That buckle is MINE.

After the gradual climb up out of Godrevy, the trail became a reasonably flat path, patches of light mud interspersed with sections of gravel. We were passed by another of the Arc 50 runners, I think the second-place person, although it could have been the third as I wasn't entirely paying attention to people passing me at speed.

Around here, up on the cliffs, is Mutton Cove, which is famed for its seal colony and at this time of year the numbers are at a peak with over one hundred seals on the beach below. I knew somewhere around Godrevy was this "seal cove" and mentioned it to Jim as we went along, but I wasn't quite sure where and had just hoped it would be obvious and we wouldn't miss it. I was wrong, and we totally missed it, although I think it may have been partly due to timing - the seals are only on the beach around low tide, but that wasn't for another 5 hours or so.

At this point, anything poking into the bottom of my shoes made those blisters shout out painfully, so I was preferring the slightly slippery mud sections to the spiky gravel path. But the worst thing I could do was stop - in 30 seconds or so the blisters seemed to inflate and then the first 5 minutes after starting walking again was a real pain in the foot.

But I had to stop at some point. Although it was a while until sunset, I had to get my headtorch out. We were making fair progress, but there was no chance of getting to the end before needing the head torch. It was also pretty windy on top of those cliffs, and although I'd covered the last 90-odd miles in just a long-sleeved merino base layer and t-shirt, with the pace dropping and wind picking up I was beginning to feel the cold.

Here was as good a place as any, so I stopped, dropped my pack off my back, and conscious of my expanding foot-blisters as quickly as possible I got my head torch out. I tucked the headlight bit into the back pocket of the bag so that I could reach round and grab it later, then had a fight with the wire and battery box, trying to get it all back into the bag. With the back of my pack zipped up I pulled the big plastic bag containing my coat and waterproof shorts out of the rear stretch pocket, causing soft flasks, a drybag, a cup and a hat to fall out. The problem with trying to do things quickly is that everything takes longer! I wrestled the coat out the bag, dropping the shorts on the ground with everything else, and put the coat on. I picked everything back up off the ground and shoved it into the now quite spacious, coat-free stuff area in the back of the pack, trying to make sure that nothing would poke in my back or stick out and catch my arm.

Job done. Jim had taken the opportunity to have a pee and I'd managed to get the majority of my faffing done at the same time, so neither of us was waiting around. Off we went.

It was nice having the coat on. On this relatively flat section of path, with no dips to hide in, the wind was continuously gusting so zipping my hood right up to the top was the only way to keep it on my head. I felt like I was wrapped in a little cocoon. The only real issue was my feet - those blisters felt like balloons and it was quite uncomfortable trying to squish them back down to pancakes over the next few minutes.

My hands were still cold, but I had the technique with the gloves now. I undid the velcro on the pole-gloves, slid them up my wrists and put on my Rab gloves, then back down with the pole-gloves and I was pole-ing along again in no time. I was all cosy now, just 3 or 4 hours of trudging through Cornwall left to do.

Up on the top of the North Cliffs, we were making reasonable progress while chatting about general nonsense. We passed places with delightful names like Hell's Mouth and Deadman's

Cove. There was a little car park just to the right of the path and I explained to Jim that my hotel was exactly 2 miles inland, a fact I knew having walked there from this very spot back in September.

We passed another car park a moment later, and I started questioning my "fact". Another car park appeared a little bit later, and I gave up spouting unsubstantiated claims about the locations of irrelevant distant buildings.

Sat on the back of an open van were a couple, waiting for their runner to come by. "Preston and Meston!" the lady shouted in a lovely Scottish accent. "I know you two as your names rhyme." I hadn't noticed. Neither had Jim. But it cheered us both and gave us something to talk about for at least the next 15 seconds. Little things, eh!

Jim kept putting in spurts. He had the idea that if he added "just 5%" then we'd get there quicker. The choice to move a bit faster would get your brain working a bit harder, legs working a bit faster, and set the tone for what was needed. It worked too - for at least 30 seconds - each time. I wasn't really feeling the extra 5%, so each time Jim sped up I lagged behind a bit, and after a few times I suggested that if he was feeling good, he should head off. He agreed, and we both laughed about the fact that at our speed we'd probably be within sight of each other for the next hour or two. I took the opportunity to empty my bladder into a bush on the edge of a cliff, building a bit of space between us, and he disappeared off into the distance as I winced my way along on foot-blisters, now having inflated as I'd stopped for a few seconds.

Passing Crane Islands on the left, it was about 4:45pm now and there was another half an hour or so before the sun set but the sky was grey and gloomy. The wind was gusty, the air wet and the moisture in the air starting to hang like light mist, but on the whole, I was fairly content now. The pace was slow, but I was working towards Portreath. You can't think longer than the next key point this late in the race, and if that key point is within a mile or two then that's just about the sort of distance my brain could handle without having some kind of a meltdown. I kept trying to ignore the 5 miles and 4 big climbs - "The Bitches" - that came after Portreath. My hood was up, I was in my own little cocoon out of the wind, the dulcet tones of Liam Gallagher singing *Champagne Supernova* to Wembley Stadium was playing in my ears.

I came to a valley. I didn't know there was a valley here. The area is Carvannel Downs, and it's really very beautiful. Legend has it that a great giant called Wrath - or Ralph - lived in a sea cave which is known as Ralph's Cupboard. He was a bit of a cheeky chappy, having a habit of wrecking passing ships, nicking their cargo and eating the sailors. Presumably he's moved now though as the top of his house has collapsed into the sea, leaving a scary but impressive drop down to the water. It was a lovely area, except for the fact that it was a valley, which meant that I had to go down the zig-zag path to the bottom, balancing on my poles and wincing more and more as I kept shocking or twisting my knee. Then across the little bridge, and back up the other side.

About half way up I had a massive sense of humour failure. On this terrain, my knee wasn't behaving at all, and every single step was painful. If it was the last hill, I would have been fine, but I was apprehensive as I knew there were 4 more hills coming up and I genuinely wasn't sure I could make it down and up them.

But... what I'd just thought: "if it was the last hill, it would be fine..." So, think no further. This *is* the last hill, and it'll be fine. I can move my legs. I can lift my knee up and get up the next step. And after that's done, I'll deal with the next step. And then the next. And I'll keep going until I get to the end. Break it down. Literally: one step at a time.

I got to the top, the path levelled off and I carried on towards Portreath. It wasn't far now, but it was starting to get dark enough to make the head torch necessary. I reached around, extracted the head-light and without stopping, spent a few minutes working out how to route the cable from the back of my vest inside my jacket hood and up to the torch on my head, which made the few hundred metres to the top of the hill down to the village pass a bit more quickly.

I carefully and slowly worked my way down the fairly steep and in places technical descent and on to the top of Battery Road which led down into Portreath. It was a nice change to be on the road, especially for those blisters on my feet, but it was a steep enough downhill to be uncomfortable to walk on and I was even more glad to head round the corner onto the flat road, the main car park being just ahead. It was 5:40pm, and it had taken me 30 minutes to cover just over a mile.

Unbeknownst to me, I'd just entered the first hedgehog friendly village in Cornwall, a fact which had I known I'm sure would have made the destination a true highlight of the course. Or... possibly not.

Portreath – 95.9 miles

2018	DNF	
2019	DNF	
2020	DNF	
2022	17:47	Target: 20:24 (2 hours 37 minutes ahead)

Competitors Remaining: 131

I had some water in my flasks and there was only 5 miles to go, but the pace I was going at made me think it would be sensible to make sure I had full supplies, so I stopped at the car park and walked around the vans looking for the Flying Angels. I couldn't see their van, but I thought I'd try my luck with someone else's crew and asked a lady who was waiting by the railings of the car park. She was so lovely! Her partner was just moving the van, and once it was in place we went round to the back and she filled up my water bottle, and offered me fruit, sweets, crisps etc. I took a packet of crisps - about the only thing I seemed to be able to stomach at the moment - thanked her, and headed off. It's true what they say about this race - everyone is bloody lovely!

I was quite worried about the next bit. I've walked and run the section of path between Porthleven and Portreath a few times in the opposite direction. The last time I was in Storming-Norman mode, and despite having covered over 20 miles so far that day I speed-walked from Porthtowan to Portreath in about 50 minutes... which wasn't a very helpful memory in the current conditions! I did remember a bit of a bitch of a climb at a place called Sally's Bottom, near Porthtowan. I also knew the very last hill up to the finish line at the Eco Park was the biggest single climb on the whole course. And a quick but thorough look at the elevation profile on my watch showed there was one more valley in the middle after the big road-climb out of Portreath. So that makes 4 more climbs, 3 more descents.

Normally, that wouldn't be a problem. I was knackered, but I've been there before and you just keep moving and get it done. But the more technical ascents and descents - and particularly those with uneven steps - were becoming a real problem for my knee.

But 5 miles. That's all. Just put one foot in front of the other.

I headed out from the car park, and followed the road in what feels like completely the wrong direction away from the coast. Knowing the area, this didn't worry me, as a few hundred metres later you curve around the back of the harbour and head back towards the sea on the north side. As I rounded the corner, I spotted the Flying Angels van - I knew there'd be one somewhere! Another particularly brilliant part of the race, the

MudCrew support was second to none. It's a difficult course, but it always feels like someone's not too far away.

Lighthouse Hill, the road up out of Portreath and so named for the old Pepperpot lighthouse on the headland, was the first hill. It wasn't too bad, a gradual climb, and the gradient was within the "comfortable" range for my knee so other than feeling a bit exhausted making my way up, it wasn't painful. The road zig-zags up, and as I was on the inside of the curve and invisible to oncoming traffic, I think I shocked a van coming down the hill, rounding the corner to see a staggering idiot on the side of the road! They didn't hit me, so I had no choice but to carry on with the race.

At the top of the hill is a big radio mast covered in all sorts of antennae, a nice marker to head towards, although not easily visible in the dark and mist as I headed up. By the top, the lighter mist of the previous section had turned into fog, and as the street lights ended and I put my head torch on I encountered a bit of a problem. The fog was reflecting almost all my head torch light, and I could see pretty much bugger all. I kept going on the right-hand side of the road with almost no visibility of the left side where I knew I'd need to join the coast path again shortly. The reflective panels on a few cars glinted in my torchlight and I headed across the road to the car park that I vaguely remembered as being an access point to the path. I hoped I was right, as I couldn't see further than a few metres ahead. Thankfully as I went along, the fog dispersed at least to the point where I could clearly see the path in patches - I was relieved as I had wondered if I was going to have to spend the whole of the last 5 miles blind!

More Arc 50 runners were coming past now, every few minutes I'd glance back and see a group of 2 or 3 lights gaining on me. I tried to be conscious of them and considerate, hugging the side of the path or easing myself out of the way so as not to hold them up, but it was getting a bit difficult to keep checking behind me and judge speed. In the end I stopped looking behind, just reacting when it was obvious there was someone behind casting a bouncing head light in my direction.

The first of those final 3 descents came half a mile after I joined the trail from the car park back at the top of Lighthouse Hill. A sharp left onto shiny, slippery rocks at the top that were quite treacherous even with poles and I had to take it very slowly, conscious again of those speedier Arc 50 runners gaining on me. The path sloped steeply down then turned to steps, that I took one at a time, making good use of my poles, and periodically squeezing into the side to let faster runners' pass.

The steps went down and down, then from the bottom there was a big, long trudge up the other side. There was a pair of chaps that I'm sure I saw more than once and I think were crewing... one was carrying a bike. Yes, a full-size mountain bike, on his shoulder, up and down some horrible, slippery, steep tracks! Fair play!

This was ascent number 1 of the final 3, and I was slowly but surely working my way up. I stopped, paused, took a breath, then took the next step. I tried a few things - does it work better if lead with the left or right leg? How about if I twist my hip? I did contemplate going up backwards, but on this dark, wet, slippery and steep path it didn't feel like the terrain to start mucking about on too much. I let a few more people pass on the way up, then I was there, at the top and now on flatter, more open terrain.

The wire fence of Portreath Remote Radar Head (RRH) caught the light of my head torch on the right side of the path just as I hit the 100-mile mark at around 6:20pm. Beyond that fence, in Nancekuke Common, the Chemical Defence Establishment had produced Sarin and VX nerve agents during the 1950s and worked towards the development of systems that could mass-produce these weapons. The site remained dormant but ready during the 60's and 70's, eventually being shut down in the 1980s, but over its lifetime produced enough chemical weapons to kill every single person on earth 5 times over. Some of the production equipment was buried on site, the rest just thrown down mine shafts. To be clear, we're talking about contaminated equipment for the production of nerve gas, just thrown down a hole in the ground. A worker digging in the area became ill in the mid-2000's, igniting media attention on the area and triggering a far more thorough clear up.

Despite its terrible history, the area beyond the fence had one thing going for it: it had also once been an airfield, and those tend to be pretty flat, a property which made its way outside the base boundary and onto the coast path on which I was walking. I kept going, walking fairly well all things considered. My memory of Sally's Bottom - the next valley - was causing me some mental issues. I had built it up to be something huge, a sheer ice-like descent down into the bowels of the Earth, then a never-ending climb of the steepest slope back up to the top. Each time my head torch light disappeared ahead, hinting at a drop, I thought "this is it!" but each time it turned out to just be a bit of a dip in the ground.

One mile after the top of the previous valley, I was finally at the top of Sally's Bottom. I tentatively headed over the top, expecting to drop away into oblivion shortly... but it never really came. It was much more zig-zagged than I remembered (which may mean that I took a much steeper route up in the dry, September daylight last time I was here). It was possibly also another case of expectation-vs-reality, making this seem easier than I'd expected. The descent was fairly easily controlled with poles, and I managed to keep my knee mostly pain free.

Then came the up. Coincidentally, someone on the South West Coast Path Facebook group had mentioned the number of steps there were up the hill in a post a few months ago, but I couldn't remember the exact number. I thought it was 60-something, but it could have been more like 80.

Looking up from the bottom, there were head torches in the sky again, a long, long way up. Ahead was the first of the steps - a new looking stone block held with 2 metal stakes. Just take one step at a time. One... two... three... I was getting used to how to drive my knee up these concrete steps: poles into the ground and a sort of rotation of the leg up onto the top of the step. It wasn't comfortable or easy, but it was mostly pain free and this was the penultimate hill, not long now.

Fifty… Sixty… Seventy… I kept counting. Occasionally, I glanced up, still seeing head torches high above. Some of the steps were pristine and new, some were almost non-existent lumps in the ground, and some looked dangerously unsupported with the large concrete block of the step seeming to be perilously close to sliding down the significant hill behind. Eighty… Ninety… One hundred. The final count was 111 steps. Just what you need with over one hundred miles in your legs!

But… it was done! One more hill and just a mile or two left to go.

Hugely relieved to be back on the flat path, I breathed a massive sigh of relief and smiled to myself. I've got this!

I passed the "bat castle" which caps the top of the 112m deep Kite's Shaft, one of the most visible mine shafts on the coast path. Someone in a group of people running near me mentioned the lights in the distance, but I didn't properly hear what they said. They carried on past and I looked around, spying some bright lights on a distant hill. Could that be the finish, the lights on the inflatable arch? Is that what he was saying?

The path was flat now, gravelly, but easy to move on. I didn't care about pain any more. I could drag myself the remainder of the distance, no blister or knee pain was going to stop me. All I wanted to do was get this thing done.

After a few minutes, there was a left turn, then a short distance further on, a car parked on the side of the path - a good sign, it meant we were nearly into the village. I took a right as shown on my watch GPS track, and a few seconds later backed out of the building site I'd just walked into, carried on a little further and took the correct right onto West Cliff, the road that heads down into Porthtowan.

I was on the road. At the bottom of this hill, I came off the South West Coast Path for the last time, to finish the last chunk of the Arc route. I was almost there.

Just down this hill. This road hill. This steep hill. This hill that's making my feet really hurt. This hill that's going on... and on... forever. This fucking hill... will it ever end?!

It did end. A few people who were obviously enjoying a beverage or two were clapping and cheering, and it was lovely! Now - with the finish guaranteed, I felt like I actually *deserved* the congratulations.

Onto the main road, I could see fluorescent jackets in the distance and as I headed towards them, I heard more "well done!" coming from pubs and car windows in the village. The Arc Angels directed me up the road, saying I should keep to the right and watch out for any cars, and that I'd be met by more marshals at the road crossing.

I knew the end was near. I knew I had one big hill to go. I had no idea of the specifics. Meeting the next set of marshals, I asked if there were any more steps - I was just hoping there weren't, and I could get up the hill with minimal knee problems. I was told there were "literally 3 steps" at the start, then no more, which was a great relief. The marshals double checked both directions were clear of juggernauts, speeding motorists and any Tour de France cyclists that had gone catastrophically wrong, and sent me across the road with instructions to follow the glow sticks.

On the left side, just across the road, was Echo Corner chimney stack - a Grade 2 listed building and the last remains of South Wheal Towan copper mine which was shut down in 1874. In August of 2019, it was almost accidentally knocked down by a couple of "young lads" under instruction from the owner! As it was 2 hours after sunset and all the light I had was coming from my head torch and pointing along the road I was heading down, the chimney passed me by completely unnoticed.

A green glowstick hanging from a bush on the right signalled the transition from road to path, and I made my way up the couple of easy steps, turning left onto the firm path. It wasn't difficult terrain, but it did go up. And up. And up. Like previous hills, I could see head torches higher up and it seemed to go on a long, long way. But the logical part of my brain - which I'm amazed was still working - told me it can't be *that* far. A few more minutes and I'd be done.

The path kept going up in more-or-less a straight line, until a sharp right. Up a wall. Or at least it seemed like it. In front of me was a step that was higher than my waist, and there was no way in hell my knee was going to make that. I tried, swore, tried again, then swore some more. Just as I was considering whether I could sort-of sit back on the step and roll backwards up the hill, I spotted a small foothold on the left-hand side. It looked a bit dodgy, but there was no other option, and I was literally minutes from the end of the race. I stuck my foot in, braced my poles in front and lurched forward, hoping like hell my shoes gripped.

And grip they did. Moments later I was on a far more sensible path, still going up though. A bit more swearing - mostly at Ferg, who I knew would be thinking this bit was the icing on the cake! - and then I climbed a stile over a small wall and was met by some smiling marshals. I asked if this was the top of the hill. "Almost, just a tiny bit to go", was the reply. And they spoke the truth - a small incline up the side of a grassy area ahead.

My watch said 7:26pm. Could I finish in the next few minutes, getting under 31.5 hours? A totally arbitrary time, but a target to push me on for the next few moments.

I saw the light from the finish arch just around the corner as another runner was in front of me sorting something out in her pack. She told me she'd be faffing for a minute and I should go on ahead. I didn't need to be asked twice. I turned into the field and broke into a limpy, pole-assisted lurching run through the finish funnel and under the arch with a race time of 31 hours, 28 minutes and 5 seconds.

Fourth time lucky. And, without a shadow of a doubt, the hardest thing I have ever done.

Finish – 100.6 miles

2018	**DNF**	
2019	**DNF**	
2020	**DNF**	
2022	**19:28**	*Target: 22:37* *(2 hours 51 minutes ahead)*

Competitors Finishing: **131**

First 3 and last 3 people who completed the race:

	Race Time	Time of Day
Mark Darbyshire	19:12:48	Sat 07:12:58
Tristan Stephenson	20:01:43	Sat 08:01:53
Dave Phillips	22:45:01	Sat 10:45:11
Luke Mclean	1d 11:09:13	Sat 23:09:23
Chris Calton	1d 11:09:24	Sat 23:09:34
Iain Walker	1d 11:12:25	Sat 23:12:35

A special mention for Iain Walker, who at 65 years of age is the oldest person to complete the Arc of Attrition, finishing in 1 day, 11 hours 12 minutes and 25 seconds.

PART 3

After the Arc

CHAPTER 12
Saturday

I had thought about the moment of crossing the finish line so many times. I'd imagined overwhelming emotions, happiness, relief and a huge sense of achievement all rolled into one.

I got none of that.

I was just numb, emotionally flat. After crossing the finish line, I got a hug from Jane (poor, poor Jane, having to hug hundreds of sweaty runners!), got handed a really impressively large and intricate matte silver buckle and someone snipped away at the tape holding my tracker and took it away.

I had a couple of photos taken where I stood and in front of the big Arc promo screen, then staggered my way into the hustle, bustle and warmth of the main area. Someone tapped me on the shoulder and congratulated me; it took me a moment to realise it was Pip! He was all changed, dressed in jeans and a jacket, having finished in a fantastic 29:09, a good couple of hours before me.

I'd promised him a lift back to the hotel while we were running, so I said to him that I'd just sort myself out a bit and then we could get going. I stood in the room in a bit of a daze, not knowing whether to just sit down or go and get my bits from the car to get changed. I opted for standing there a bit more, then spied Stephen Cousins by the entrance.

I wandered over, and told him that I'd finished, this time explaining who the hell I was by mentioning that it was my fourth attempt and I'd finally finished the bloody thing! Ten seconds later, I'm in front of the camera with him explaining who I was and asking how it all went. I don't remember much about that moment; I look back at that interview and wonder how I put together any coherent sentences!

I went back inside and stood around again, still trying to will my brain into making a decision about what to do when a chap said that there was a "competitors' area" out the back where I could just sit down, get a cup of tea and have a rest. That sounded nice... so I happily followed on and got myself a seat in a room full of shell-shocked people sitting on chairs.

I had a quick chat with Jim Preston - he'd got himself lost somewhere on the route and despite going on ahead of me before Portreath had actually finished 55 seconds behind me.

I had a cup of tea with sugar in it, and chilled out for a bit. The blisters on my feet were sore, and the medics were offering to help but I didn't see much point as I'd only be able to put back on the manky, wet socks I'd take off as everything clean was back in the car. I just thought I'd wait until I got back to the hotel room and sort it out there.

After a few conversations I don't really remember, I got my drop back that had been brought back from the Land's End checkpoint, picked up my car key, said thank you to everyone and headed back out of the room, greedily eyeing some pizza on the side until I realised it wasn't checkpoint food but a proper takeaway pizza someone had ordered - I'm pretty sure they wouldn't have been very happy if I'd helped myself to a load of it!

I stood in the main area, looking around all the people and trying to spot Pip. As I stood there, I felt the blood draining from my head and had to quickly find a spot to sit down before I fell over. A moment with my head between my legs and I was back together again.

On standing up again, I spotted Pip and we headed out of the building towards the car park, Pip walking normally, with me waddling like a very slow penguin. Back at the car, I stripped off shoes, gaiters and 2 pairs of socks, replacing them with a clean pair of both socks and shoes. It felt so nice!

I drove very carefully the 5 or 6 miles to Camborne Travelodge. The hotel is on the same site as a KFC, Dominos and Costa with a McDonalds just across the road. I was really starting to feel hungry, but I didn't know what I wanted... that pizza back at the HQ had looked very good and I quite fancied a Dominos. But that would have meant walking across the car park and waiting for 10 minutes… and KFC was just there, in front of me.

I said goodbye to Pip who was heading back to his hotel with a promise to meet up when he's next down my neck of the woods, and headed to KFC. 5 minutes later I was back in the car with a box of fast food. I decided to take it back to the room, so drove the mile or so back to my hotel, left all the sweaty and stinking stuff in the back of the car and headed in with a couple of bags of clothes and my KFC.

As I got to the entrance, a woman was outside the door having a cigarette. She gave me a well done as I staggered my way up to the doorway, saying that her husband had finished as well in a little under 30 hours. I congratulated him, via her, and headed inside.

Through reception, I got to the bottom of the stairs. Despite having been to this hotel about 10 times before, I'd never used the lift, but I assumed there must be one somewhere so I had a look back out into reception to see if I could spot the familiar steel doors. Nope. Oh well, I couldn't be bothered to go on a hunt for it so just single-stepped my way up the staircase to the first floor and headed along to my room.

I ate the food like someone that hadn't eaten for a week.

The great thing about most Premier Inn hotels is that the bathroom has a bath. I set the taps going with lukewarm water and stripped everything off, cringing at the state of my blister-ridden feet and the red-raw patches all over my back where my pack had been rubbing.

I stepped into the bath and immediately jumped back out again. Despite it really not being very hot, it felt like I'd just stepped into molten lava! It took me a minute or two to acclimatise my feet to the water, and eventually I lowered myself in, wincing as each new blister, scrape or rubbed patch met the water. As I sat there, everything hurt. I just hoped it was doing some good.

After a while, I drained the bath and looked down at my filthy, mud-covered legs. Well, the bath had felt relaxing in the end, but I wasn't clean, so I had a shower and cleaned as best I could without causing too much pain to toes, legs and back.

I was feeling completely exhausted now, and just wanted to go to bed. It was about 9:30pm, I hadn't slept for about 39 hours and had covered 103 miles on foot, so I think that was perfectly reasonable!

I tried to drink lots of water, but it's difficult when all you get is a teeny, tiny little hotel-room glass. Why do they do that? After downing 4 glasses, my stomach complained so I gave up.

Just before getting into bed, I took a photo of my buckle so I could stick it on the Strava track and that would be on my phone. I opened Strava, but it wasn't there - not unusual, the watch often doesn't sync to the phone without a poke. I opened the Garmin Connect app, and sync'd. It took a couple of seconds, then told me it was done. Still no track. I looked on my watch at the most recent run… and it was a 10-mile run from the previous Monday. My weekly total sat at 10 miles.

The only conclusion I could come to at that moment was that instead of hitting *Save* on my watch after I'd finished, I'd accidentally hit *Discard*. I thought I'd be gutted, having just lost the track for such a personally important run. But, like with the finish, I was just emotionally flat… I didn't care.

I stuck a quick post on Instagram of my buckle and a comment about losing the track and having nothing to put on Strava, then lay down and switched the light off. I hoped for a relaxing, recuperating sleep, but knew that wouldn't happen.

I was right. I tossed and turned and wrestled with the duvet for what felt like hours. My legs were sore. My back was sore. My head was sore. At about 3am, I woke up absolutely ravenous and put the light on, lying awake. I phoned reception to ask about booking a spot for breakfast, but they were full. I had a quick look on my phone and decided I'd go to Wetherspoons in town tomorrow - they opened at 7am, so I set my alarm for 6:45am and tried to get a little more sleep.

CHAPTER 13
Sunday

Getting out of bed the morning after a hilly 100 miler is not a pleasant experience. First, there's the realisation that you can't just lay there any more, that you're going to have to actually move. Then there's getting those sleepy, stiff and painful legs over the edge of the bed and up into a seating position, letting the wave of dizziness pass.

Then there's standing up, on those lovely inflated blisters. The first 5 minutes of walking around the room was absolute hell! My legs would hardly move, and every step hurt as the blisters compressed. But the more I moved, the better it felt, to the point of just about being able to move. I made a crap instant coffee to celebrate having made it as far as the kettle, and then very carefully got some clothes and shoes on.

I got to thinking about the activity I'd deleted from my watch. I figured there might be a couple of ways of recovering it if the data was still actually on the watch, which it should be. I had my laptop in my rucksack, so I picked that up and headed out the door.

I drove the 0.9 miles to Wetherspoons and willed there to be a parking space nearby. The universe was on my side - directly opposite was a layby and as I approached, a van pulled out leaving me a nice easy space to park in with no Sunday parking restrictions. I slowly headed over the crossing into a pretty empty Wetherspoons at 7:56am on a Sunday morning.

I picked a corner booth and dug out my phone. When your legs don't work, it's nice to be able to order stuff on an app, and 'Spoons have got that working perfectly. I added a coffee to the basket on the app, then headed to the breakfast section. The full English breakfast was unavailable! What?! Nooooo! A bit more of a dig around on the menu and some deductive skills suggested that they'd just run out of sausages, so I ordered a vegetarian breakfast with a side of black pudding and bacon.

I'd forgotten that the coffee comes as an empty cup and I had to walk across the whole pub to get to the machine, but my legs were actually starting to feel a bit more like they would behave. It was slow, but not uncomfortable, and moving actually felt like it was doing some good.

My breakfast arrived as I was digging into the file system on my watch from my computer, and I tucked into the food while poking around in various folders on the watch. I backed up the whole watch, then took a look around and found a FIT file that was much bigger than the others. Opening it in a map viewer, I was overjoyed to see it was my Arc track! I couldn't understand why it hadn't synchronised to my watch, until a bit more investigation showed that in fact it *had*, it was just classified as a *walk* instead of a *run*, so hadn't shown up in the list. A bit rude, I thought - I'd run at least some of it! I twiddled the settings and hey presto, my weekly mileage jumped to 113, and Strava showed me the track and charts in all their glory.

I couldn't finish all the food. I was incredibly hungry, but there wasn't enough room in my stomach to put it all in. I got another coffee, and sat back with the laptop writing up some notes and thoughts about the race.

I spoke to my sister who suggested I get some antiseptic cream for my back, so I decided to wait in the pub until 10am when the Aldi across the road would open. I carried on writing some nonsense on the computer and drinking coffee to pass the time, content and relaxed in the corner of the pub.

Aldi was busy when I went in. I couldn't find any antiseptic cream, but picked up another box of paracetamol and 3 beers and headed back to the car.

On the way home, I made a mistake at a roundabout. I changed my mind about the direction I was going to go at the last second, and ended up pulling out in front of someone. It was all very slow, there was no drama, but I hate making driving mistakes and that was a big one that could have ended in a prang. I carefully drove the mile or so back to the hotel, very glad that I wasn't doing the 200-odd mile journey home today, and decided no more driving until tomorrow.

My wife and kids had given me a gift bag to have after I'd finished the race, but it had been in the car overnight as I'd forgotten to take it out. Back in the room now, I was enjoying a mini bottle of Prosecco and munching some tangy Colin the Caterpillar sweets which were going down particularly well.

The raw patch on my back has been painful in the night, and digging around in my various first aid kits I found a big dressing and some micropore tape and patched it up. I also found a JointAce patch in a bag, it's a sort of pain-reduction, herbal healing patch to target joint pain. I'd bought them after someone recommended them for aches and pains that I might get during the South West Coast Path walk, but never used them. I figured I might as well give it a go now, and stuck it onto the sore bit of my knee. I'm not sure if it did any good, but it did feel nice.

I went back to bed and set the alarm for 3 hours. I think I got about 20 minutes of sleep and then gave up.

Something had been niggling me. I've got this step streak going - I've done a minimum of 7,500 steps every day for the last 1,350 days. Now, I could bend the rule a bit, and say that I did 202,000 steps over the previous 2 days and let myself off - like a sensible, normal, person would. But then it occurred to me that if I walked the mile to Wetherspoons and back, I could (a) get some food, (b) get some steps, and (c) get some beer, all of which seemed like a good idea. And, from past experience, I was pretty sure the movement would help my legs return to normal faster.

So, I grabbed my rucksack, stuffed in a down jacket and Minimus waterproof jacket just in case and headed out the door, wobbling my way the mile or so to the pub. As I got close, I realised I wouldn't do enough steps, so I added a 10-minute extra walk around the block before heading in to the pub. As predicted, it was certainly loosening my legs up and by the end I was walking relatively normally, just not very quickly.

Two Doom Bars, an Empire State burger (2,000 calories!) and a few more thousand words of notes on the laptop and I was staggering back out the door like someone who'd had way too many beers… into the pouring rain. It was lucky I'd packed my rain jacket!

As I turned into the hotel car park, my watch buzzed to say I'd completed my step goal. Back in the room, I had a wash and went straight to bed, despite it being before 8pm. But sleep did not come, and at 11pm I sat at the table, feeling very hungry still, drinking the final beer bottle and having some more paracetamol in the hope that I would get to sleep soon.

CHAPTER 14

Monday

Today, I go home. 178 miles of driving, and I've had another terrible night sleep. It's 7:15am, and I just want to sleep for the rest of the day.

My Garmin has this "Body Battery" measurement, which uses heart-rate variability to determine a stress level, and then uses the stress level to deplete a kind-of virtual battery representing your overall health and energy. Mine hit the bottom (5%) on Saturday evening. And it's still there. It usually goes up to somewhere between 60 and 90% after a normal night's sleep, but it's just sat, flatlining at 5%. I'd say it's pretty representative of how I'm feeling.

I left the hotel about 8:30am, stuck the car on charge and wobbled my way around the corner to McDonalds for a McBreakfast of some variety. After a muffin and a coffee, I drove 101 miles to Dart's Farm, stuck the car on charge again (I'm lucky - mine's free to charge so I make the most of it!), and got more caffeine and a steak pasty.

I got home mid-afternoon, hoping that a veil of peace and relaxation would descend upon me and I'd sleep like a log in my own bed.

For the third night, I had another shit sleep. My feet and lower legs were constantly in pain, and it was impossible to get comfortable in bed. I headed to the lounge at 4am and wrote more of this nonsense down.

During the day on Tuesday, I had a bit of a sleep and finally started to feel a bit more human, with my legs a little less painful now it was 60 hours since I'd finished.

I'm finally processing the event. I feel happier, and I'm genuinely pleased I've finished, but I have no inclination to do it again, unlike previous years. I've got the Oner in April - I'm a bit worried about that now as it's a long way with a tight cutoff, but I think I'll have a break from long distance stuff after that. I've got no desire to get out again at the moment, I can happily ignore the coast path and not have to visit Cornwall again for a long time!

As I was daydreaming about things, my phone went ping. What's this…?

Facebook:

"A reminder that the 2022 RAT inc the middle distance British Trail Running Championships 50k opens for entries tonight at 6PM , early entry is always advised as the event sells out well in advance."